D0282574

FROM THE AUTHOR:

THIS IS NOT ONLY MY SON ILAN'S STORY. I want it to be published to remind people of what hatred and intolerance can do, hatred for the other, intolerance of what we see as different. Given the world we live in today, we have to remember that we are all people, and we are the same, regardless of our beliefs. Otherwise, there will be very dark times ahead.

—*Ruth Halimi*

FROM THE HEADLINES:

PRINCETON, N.J. (Mar. 2016)—Neo-Nazi Andrew Auernheimer hacks into printers at universities around the country, sending out a raft of hateful, anti-Semitic propaganda...

CHARLOTTESVILLE, Va. (Aug. 2017)—For two days this college town rang with racist, anti-Semitic chants, as white supremacists gathered to make their bigotry known publicly...

LYONS, Ill. (Mar. 2018)—Arthur Jones, longtime Holocaust denier and former head of the American Nazi Party, wins the Republican nomination for the Third Congressional District of Illinois...

PITTSBURGH (Oct. 2018)—At 9:50 a.m., in the midst of Saturday services, Robert Bowers, armed with an assault rifle and three handguns, burst into the Tree of Life Synagogue in Pittsburgh's Squirrel Hill neighborhood shouting, "All Jews must die!"...

POWAY, Calif. (Apr. 2019)—On a quiet Sabbath morning, a young man armed with an AR-15-style gun stormed into the Chabad synagogue, shouting anti-Semitic slurs...

The Kidnapping and Murder of Ilan Halimi

Ruth Halimi

Émilie Frèche

Translated by Renuka George

Foreword by Jonathan Greenblatt, Anti-Defamation League

Behrman House

www.behrmanhouse.com

Original French edition published under the title *24 Jours*

Published by Behrman House, Inc.
Millburn, New Jersey
www.behrmanhouse.com

ISBN: 978-1-68115-008-6

Cover image: Shutterstock/Marcos Mesa Sam Wordley
Photo of Ilan Halimi (back flap) courtesy of Jeremy Chlouch

Developmental Editor: Diana Drew
Copy Editor: Judith Sandman
Project Manager: Terry S. Kaye
Design: Neustudio, Inc.

The publisher gratefully acknowledges Jessica Reaves, Anti-Defamation League, for writing the news vignettes and Todd Gutnick, Anti-Defamation League, for his invaluable help with the project.

To protect the privacy of individuals who are not public figures, the following pseudonyms have been used in place of real names, and any similarity between these names and existing names is unintended and purely coincidental: Frederic Arnaud, Orville Aubert, Marcel Caron, Jacques Durand, Martin Durand, Karl Fouad, Jaimie Garnier, Pauline Girard, Jules Huet, Monique Joly, Renée Jouer, Maurice Keller, Jean Loiselle, Aimée Nicolas, Gabriel Petit, Rabbi Théo Zarquette.

Library of Congress Cataloging-in-Publication data can be found at the end of this book.

Printed in the United States of America

9 8 7 6 5 4 3 2 1

Contents

Foreword

I ALWAYS WILL remember Ilan Halimi.

When I first heard about his murder in 2006 I was living in Los Angeles, shuttling to Seattle, where I was working at a Fortune 500 company. I remember reading the harrowing account of his murder at work. I pulled back from my desk, dazed. This wasn't the kind of story that would retreat to some corner of my mind to be forgotten. It felt seared onto my soul.

First, there was the event itself. It almost seemed inexplicable, like something out of a horror movie. The notion of a young man kidnapped, tortured, and killed by a band of thugs.

None of the details were clear, but it instantly hit me hard: he was murdered because he was a Jew.

Perhaps it hit home because my grandparents were born in Europe. They escaped the Nazi death machine, but most of their relatives were slaughtered in the Holocaust. The continent remained a place where Jews could end up being killed simply because they were Jewish. Ilan was yet another name added to a long list.

Perhaps it hit home because my wife still has family in France. They live every day with the kind of fear engendered by persistent, pervasive anti-Semitism. One day I suspect that they will flee, eager to spare their children the fate that befell Ilan.

Whatever it may have been, the news of the murder seized me. It has stayed with me and been a source of pain for nearly a decade. It imprinted itself on my conscience, the kind of far-off event that would remain with me forever.

And so, when I accepted the CEO role at the Anti-Defamation League in late 2014, I made myself a personal promise: I would seek out the Halimi family. I would connect with them and grieve for their son. And I would open myself to them. I would do so because, while I couldn't reverse the horrible course of events that stole Ilan's life, I could ensure that our organization, one that is charged with fighting anti-Semitism, would do whatever it could for a family who lost their son to this ancient hatred.

Thus, when I met Ruth Halimi, Ilan's mother, on my first visit to France in 2015, it turned out to be one of the most meaningful moments of my life.

It took some time to set the meeting. Ruth Halimi is not a public celebrity. She has little appetite for attention. In fact, she is an intensely private person who intentionally has shunned the spotlight, a sign of her quiet dignity.

Our meeting was arranged with the help of the local Jewish Federation in Paris. We met in an unassuming building in the early afternoon. After we were buzzed in and crossed the foyer, we were greeted by a small woman with kind eyes. Ruth is somewhat frail; she slowly extended her hand, but instantly she radiated a quiet kind of steadiness and almost familiarity. I immediately felt as if I knew her.

As we met, she looked directly into my eyes. I could see the lines on her face, the tiredness. I reached over and took her hand in mine. She had suffered so much, grieved for so long, and yet she appeared to carry her almost unspeakable burden with solemnity and strength.

It was difficult to communicate. Her English was negligible, and I speak little French. But we understood each other, a kind of mutual respect and shared awareness of what it means to be Jewish and to raise Jewish children in a world that is often unsafe for them.

We spoke for several hours. At the end of our conversation, Ruth pulled out a manila envelope. She had brought a manuscript. It was her story and that of her son, albeit published in French. She asked if we could help her to get it published in English in the United States.

I grasped it close to my chest. It felt heavy in my hands. I held Ruth's gaze and promised her that we would do just that.

And that is the book you now hold in your hands.

It is the story of yet another Jewish martyr, a man who died like so many before him simply because of the heritage into which he was born. It is a reminder of the hate that lurks around the corner, that is on the rise, and that will cause irreparable harm if given a chance.

And yet Ruth's story is important not just as another sad chapter in Jewish or French history—it is also significant as a reminder of what can happen anywhere or to anyone when hatred is left unchecked. Ilan's kidnapping took place because anti-Semitism has been able to persist throughout history, to span across countries and cultures, with too few people speaking out and striving to stop it. It is characterized by a set of conspiracy theories and sinister tropes about Jews: that they are clannish, controlling, greedy, manipulative, and like to hoard money.

Since Ilan's death, there have been numerous other violent anti-Semitic incidents in France and across Europe. And similar acts are happening around the world with increasing frequency. In recent years, we have seen an alarming rise of anti-Semitism and white supremacy here in the US, with extremists increasingly asserting themselves in public life and violating our sacred spaces—think of recent episodes in communities like Charleston, Charlottesville, Pittsburgh, Poway.

I don't believe that we can afford to dismiss these spasms of violence as unconnected outliers. In contrast, they strike me as data points on a trend line, one that is enabled by the enduring filament of age-old anti-Semitism.

They also underscore the fact that hatred doesn't stop at the door of the Jews. Anti-Semitism is not a Jewish problem per se.

It is a universal one, because, if it is not snuffed out, this kind of bigotry can catch fire like kindling and metastasize into an inferno that eventually will consume all in its path.

We can't bring justice to Ilan, but this book is dedicated to him and every other Ilan—every Jew singled out because of his or her faith, every person demonized because of difference. In his death, let us hope that Ilan Halimi can enjoy the peace that was stolen from him. And let us lock arms with Ruth and every other parent who has lost a son or a daughter to cruelty and hate. We owe it to them and ultimately to our own children to use all our might to interrupt and extinguish this kind of intolerance before it erupts again.

Jonathan Greenblatt
CEO and National Director
Anti-Defamation League
New York

Preface

In 2006, Ilan Halimi, a young French citizen, was kidnapped, tortured, and put to death because he was a Jew. *24 Days*, written by Ilan's mother, Ruth, with the help of my friend Émilie Frèche, tells his tragic story.

Ilan was a son of France. He could have been my brother, my cousin, or my nephew. He was killed for one reason: because he was Jewish. He was killed out of hatred, stupidity, and prejudice: the kidnappers were convinced that he was rich simply because he was Jewish. Ilan's death marks the tragic revival of murderous anti-Semitism in France.

We will never forget Ilan. His name has become the symbol of our determination to fight anti-Semitism. That is why I've created a national prize in Ilan's name, rewarding projects created by young people to fight anti-Semitism and racism. Frèche, with the consent of Ilan's family, has agreed to serve as president of the jury.

I was humbled and privileged to meet Ruth Halimi. She encouraged us to combat all forms of hatred with all of our strength. As prime minister of France, fighting the scourge of anti-Semitism is a moral and political imperative. Anti-Semitism is the negation of the very values for which the French Republic stands. My government is fully committed to prosecuting any person who carries out anti-Semitic acts and to educating the population against hatred. In this fight against hatred, ignorance, cowardice, and impunity, I know I can rely on all the French people who love their country and the values of universality and fraternity. Sadly, anti-Semitism is spreading not only throughout Europe but around the world. I know we can count on our American friends to fight this fight together and defend the common values we cherish.

Édouard Philippe
Prime Minister of France

A Mother's Duty

The freezing damp penetrates our bones and forces us to lower our heads as we walk. The pale rays of the rising sun are powerless against this winter morning. I would have wanted to be able to stand erect, but we have to watch our step as our shoes sink into the mud. It's been raining all week long. The pathways in the cemetery have melted into the tombs. We're scared of slipping and move slowly through the darkness, holding hands, like a band of outlaws.

Why had the time for the exhumation of Ilan's body been set for dawn? Couldn't we have taken him out of here in broad daylight, with everyone watching? I would have liked the world to see us exhuming my son, who had been murdered at the age of twenty-three, but the police had asked us to come today, Wednesday, February 7, 2007, at six in the morning. Ilan will leave Pantin Cemetery just as he left his life, without any fuss. When they found him, still breathing, about a year ago, he couldn't even say his name. He was lying naked beside a train track; the only sound he uttered was a gasp. His head was shaven, his hands were bound, and his whole body was covered in burn marks. Two policemen said to me, "Madam, nobody would do what they did to him, not even to an animal."

✦

His headstone is the twenty-first in the third row in Sycamore Alley. Finally, we reach our destination and try to form a small circle around it. The "inner circle"—the family, the best friends, the men and women Ilan liked to have around him when he was blowing out the candles to celebrate another year of his life—that's all over now. How can we possibly be here for him, on this terribly cold and dark morning, without him? How is it possible?

The rabbi launches into a prayer. He's singing, but it sounds to me as if he's crying, his voice is so weak. Unless it's my own sobs that are distorting his voice. I can hear them echoing within me, and, to hold them back, I clench my fists, tucked deep into my pockets. I want to remain dignified—that's all I have left.

I gaze out into the distance. I stare at the small squares of light that appear here and there in the rows of buildings that block the horizon; I imagine them to be hundreds of lamps burning for Ilan. Everywhere else the night lingers on. So hostile that it forces us to curtail this ceremony. The rabbi speeds up the service, and his words fly off to be absorbed by the hum of the city that reaches us in snatches on the wind. There's no tranquility in this cemetery in Paris, no peace, no silence, just a constant dull rumble that never allows the dead to rest. This is certainly the reason I wanted to bury Ilan in Jerusalem.

I wanted to do it right away, right at the beginning; it made the most sense to me. But his father and sisters didn't see things that way. They wanted to keep him close, to be able to visit him every time they felt the need. So Ilan was buried here, in Pantin, on Friday, February 17, 2006.

That day, hundreds of people had come to bid him a last farewell. Maybe there were a thousand people present. There were so many unfamiliar faces, so many others whom I hadn't seen for years . . . I think each of them was thinking of their son, their brother. Yes, every one of them must have imagined their child, instead of mine, in this coffin. Ripples of dread were running through the crowd.

I came back to Ilan's grave in March, April, May, and then every month until this day, his first *yahrtzeit*, the anniversary of his death. I never abandoned the idea of transferring his remains to Israel. I felt it was my duty as a mother to accord Ilan the peace I didn't believe he could find here, in this land where he was starved, beaten, wounded, burned. How could you rest in peace in a country where you had suffered so much? This question, that neither my daughters nor my ex-husband was capable of answering, finally convinced us that Jerusalem should be his last resting place.

✦

Two silhouettes that had remained in the background all this time walk toward the grave, and I wonder who these men are. Family? Friends? Just gravediggers, who have come to dig up my son with their spades.

Each thud feels like a contraction, and they churn my stomach so violently that, for a moment, I stupidly believe Ilan is going to emerge from the earth as he emerged from my body. I tell myself to stand firm, to be brave. My eyes remain glued to the two boys who pull on the ropes to raise Ilan's coffin. I hear the wood bang against the sides of the vault, and, just as on the day he was born,

I have to scream to alleviate the pain. Yes, I scream. With all my might. With my whole soul. But the cries of a mother giving birth are nothing like the screams of a mother exhuming her son: The latter bring no relief.

✦

Ilan's coffin finally reaches the surface. I watch in disbelief as the long box swings past our faces, like a gigantic shadow. Can my child really be inside it? The child I carried, gave birth to, breastfed? Can that body really be a corpse now?

The undertakers shove the coffin into the hearse, and the doors shut with a metallic clang. The vehicle starts up slowly, then moves off, moves off, moves off . . . and I think, that's it, it's over. Ilan is leaving. Ilan is leaving Paris; he's leaving France. And you who murdered him—you won't be able to hurt him anymore. That's the reason I came to get him. Now I know why I took him away from here: because they'll end up being released from prison one day and could come to spit on his grave.

February 27, 2017

PHILADELPHIA—The desecration of Jewish cemeteries and gravestones has communities on edge in Missouri and Pennsylvania. Vandals have targeted Jewish cemeteries near Philadelphia and in St. Louis, toppling hundreds of headstones and leaving grieving family and community members to pick up the pieces. The bleak history of such attacks was not lost on Rebecka Hess of West Philadelphia. "I'm a child of a Holocaust survivor, so I grew up with stories of destruction of Jewish cemeteries," she told Philadelphia's television station WPVI. "I always thought we were done with that."

Just Another Friday Evening

It's a lovely winter's day. The sales have just begun, and the excited crowds impart a lively atmosphere to the city. I use my lunch hour to go shopping, and at André I find a pair of boots for Ilan. I'd noticed some others, nicer ones, in the window of a shoe store on the way to work, but they cost a fortune, and I couldn't afford them. I hope he'll like these, since you can't exchange anything bought on sale. The saleswoman tells me I'd do better to come back with my son, but I worry they may no longer have his size, so I just buy them for him.

✦

This Friday, like every Friday, I leave my office early. I stop at the supermarket to buy a few bits and pieces for the evening, then hurry home to prepare Shabbat dinner. It's a ritual I wouldn't give up for anything in the world; since my children have grown up, it's only at this meal that I have a chance to spend some quiet time with them. Eve and Ilan still live with me, but they are twenty-five and twenty-three, respectively. They have their own lives. During the week our interactions are fleeting. As for Deborah, my twenty-four-year-old daughter, she no longer lives with us. She got married two years ago and has given me a lovely granddaughter, Noa.

We've lived in the same apartment forever, on the second floor of an old building, in a working-class area in the east of Paris. It's a simple, two-bedroom apartment; the children have to share a room, but we're happy here. This is where Deborah, Eve, and Ilan grew up; they enjoy living in this lively area of the capital with its diverse population.

As I walk up the avenue loaded down with shopping bags, between the bare branches of a chestnut tree my eyes instinctively seek out our living-room window. I'm hoping to catch a glimpse of Ilan. When he gets home first, he watches for me and comes down to help carry my packages upstairs. His father had left when he was two, so Ilan's more or less the man of the house . . . Today the balcony is empty, and suddenly I remember that, just two weeks ago, my son had gone back to his former job at a cell-phone store on boulevard de Magenta. He only finishes work at 7:00 p.m., so there's no chance of my finding him at home in the middle of the afternoon.

The apartment is, in fact, deserted, and I use these few hours alone to set to work. Shabbat is a celebration. It's the most beautiful day, the day the Jews welcome, as a fiancé welcomes his beloved, with joy and enthusiasm. Although I'm not an orthodox follower of the faith, I respect this rite. It gives me the opportunity to set a beautiful table, to gather my family around me, and to prepare the dishes my grandmother used to make for me—recipes that taste of Morocco, my homeland. It takes me a while to get the meal ready, and I'm still engrossed in my cooking when Eve slips her key into the lock.

My older daughter looks just like Ilan; when they were kids people thought they were twins. Both have jet-black hair, sparkling eyes, and smiles that make their faces light up. All the same, Eve is much smaller than her brother. She's home early because she's looking for a job in human resources. Even though she's sent out dozens of résumés, she hasn't had many responses. Of course she's worried.

"Aren't Deborah and David coming for dinner?" she asks, noticing the three places laid at the table.

"No. Your sister called five minutes ago. She'd rather not go out tonight. We'll have lunch at their place tomorrow."

✦

Ilan arrives a few minutes later, at about 7:15, 7:30. I don't know if it's because he's the only man in the house, but as soon as he enters, it feels as if the place comes to life again. The apartment is now filled with familiar sounds, including his voice, which is louder than ours. Like all young people, my son scatters bits of himself in every room—his cell phone, his keys, the words of the latest hit he hums.

"Where's Noa?" he asks, noticing his little niece's absence.

"Don't look so upset. You'll see her tomorrow," Eve replies.

A faint scowl of disappointment clouds Ilan's face, and, as always, Eve and I smile. Ilan takes off his leather jacket then comes to join us in the living room. Mechanically, I ask him how his day went. He doesn't look anxious, but I can imagine that he isn't overjoyed at having gone back to work as a salesman. He only decided to do this because he feels it's time to earn a proper living. The salary at the real estate company where he'd worked before had been very low, and he was tired of never being able to buy himself anything.

"So, how was your day?" I ask.

Ilan shrugs, as if to say, Nothing special. He doesn't tell me he'd filled in for someone at his boss's other shop on boulevard Voltaire. Nor does he mention the pretty brunette who had come into the shop just to ask him for his cell number. Why would he tell me about it? It's certainly not the first time he's had a girl flirt with him, and anyway, he has a girlfriend . . . Ilan's been going out with Mony for over a year now. She's a lovely Asian girl who lives a stone's throw from our apartment. I've only met her two or three times, but I think my son has grown attached to her. In any case, he sleeps over at her place more often than he does at ours.

✦

"I don't understand why you went back to this job. Last year you were saying that the phone business wasn't right for you. You resigned yourself to start working in real estate, and you're going back to phones now?""I don't have a choice," replies Ilan, irritated by the conversation.

I should keep quiet, let him live his own life, but I'm sure he's just wasting his time. So I insist: "Why don't you call your father? He could lend you a bit of money to start your own business." My son doesn't want to ask anyone for anything, not even his father; he wants to do everything himself. He wants us to be proud of him, and he dismisses my suggestions with a joke. We shift to the table.

Ilan sets his *kippah* on his head. He only wears it on Friday evenings, to say the Shabbat prayers, and for the major festivals. He isn't religious, but he was brought up according to tradition: He knows the texts. We listen as he sings the Kiddush, then, after him, we sip the wine. Ilan leaves us to go and wash his hands, as prescribed in the rite, and when he returns, he launches into the blessing over the bread. He cuts off small pieces, which he dips in the salt; he puts one into his mouth and passes the others to us. We wish each other "Shabbat shalom." A peaceful Shabbat.

We have a pleasant dinner, but I feel as if it ends too soon. Maybe because there were just the three of us—we were missing Deborah, her husband, David, and their little Noa. It was a Friday that could have been a Monday, an ordinary meal that didn't have the fragrance of a celebration . . .

By 9:00 p.m. we'd already left the table. Ilan checked his emails and made a few phone calls.

Later I would say he seemed irritated, anxious. I would scour my memory for the smallest detail that could have served as a warning, but, in reality, nothing that evening could have foretold what was about to happen to him. Ilan's somewhat exasperated, but it's only because his plans for the evening aren't working out. Mony, whom he was planning to meet, is still at work. As for Karim and Jérémie, his two best friends, they have no desire to go anywhere. In passing, I hear Ilan trying to convince them over the phone: "Come on, just for a while. Are you guys old men, or what? We won't be back late . . ."

When I see my son shrugging his jacket on again, I can't help reminding him that it's Friday night. However much I tell myself that he isn't a child anymore, and he can do what he wants, I don't like him going out on Shabbat. Ilan knows this, but he's young, he has to meet someone, and he can't be bothered with religious taboos that remind him of his mother as he's about to set off . . . Mom, you don't really mind, do you? says his small guilty smile. Then I see him turn, and, to hold on to him, to keep him there a few seconds longer, as if I had a premonition this would be the last time, I ask him to try on the boots I bought for him. "Now, right away, this instant? Tomorrow," Ilan promises, and the door shuts on the kisses he sends me. From afar.

Day 1 ....

The Nightmare Begins

A Puzzling Absence

"Is Ilan back?"

"No, he must have slept over at Mony's," replies Eve, who's just woken up.

"Why don't you call him? I'm sure he's forgotten that we're having lunch at Deborah's."

My daughter immediately picks up her phone. She's connected to his voice mail and leaves a message for him. We both spend the morning at home. Then, toward midday, we set off for David and Deborah's. They live in a small apartment in the inner Parisian suburbs, where they moved when the baby was born. By car it's not far from where we live, but I don't drive during Shabbat, so we walk.

Noa greets us on all fours, in the doorway, at the entrance. My granddaughter can barely utter three garbled words, but she already knows how to say her uncle's name. She repeats it over and over again when she sees us. She's asking for him.

We wait quite a while for Ilan before sitting down at the table. We try several times to contact him, but we keep getting his voice mail. He probably went to bed late and is still asleep. So we decide to start without him. I keep telling myself that he'll join us whenever he gets here, but I'm still somewhat annoyed that he hasn't kept his promise. He had promised to be here. And then I forget my disappointment . . . My granddaughter, whose every gesture captivates me, holds my full attention.

The lunch conversation is good-humored, despite the strange phone call David receives in the middle of the meal. He mumbles a few words of excuse and goes off into the bedroom for some privacy. It must be a professional call . . . My son-in-law works in real estate; his clients call him at all hours, even on weekends—we don't make an issue of it. However, when he returns, his face has changed.

"Is everything okay?" asks his wife, concerned.

"Yes, yes, everything's fine," he replies, unconvincingly. David waits until I've left the table with Noa to speak to Eve and Deborah.

"It was Mony," he says to them. "She's terribly worried. She hasn't heard from Ilan."

"He didn't sleep at her place?" asks Eve, surprised.

"No, he didn't come back all night. She spoke to him at about 10:30. He told her he was meeting one of his colleagues from work—someone called Gabriel Petit—and since then, nothing. He isn't answering his messages or his texts."

"He must have spent the evening with Karim or Jérémie," Deborah suggests.

"No, Mony's called them. They didn't see Ilan last night."

"Well, it's not that serious, is it?" asks Deborah, seeking reassurance.

"I don't know," says David. "I find it a bit strange."

"Stop!" Eve scolds. "He must have been partying; I'm sure he fell asleep at a friend's place . . ."

✦

Despite my daughters' apparent calm, David isn't convinced. He tells us that he has to show an apartment and leaves the house. In reality, he goes straight to our local police station. Maybe Ilan's in some kind of trouble—who knows? Maybe he's been arrested; maybe he's had an accident.

The police know nothing at all. They didn't stop anyone with Ilan's name last night, but they suggest that David contact the hospitals. All the hospitals my son-in-law calls that afternoon say the same thing: "We don't have the name Ilan Halimi in our records." But David doesn't give up. He questions a few of my son's friends to find out if anyone's heard from him. Nobody has. Not even Mony. Still no news.

By now, David is seriously worried. While his brother-in-law often stays out late and sleeps elsewhere, David knows him, and it isn't like him not to answer his phone or to miss a family meal for no reason and without an apology.

Back at home David shares his concern with my daughters. The anxiety slowly sinks in, but I remain oblivious to what's going on around me. Throughout the three interminable weeks of this nightmare, my children constantly try to protect me.

✦

Darkness fell a while ago. I'm still at my son-in-law and daughter's place; it must be 7:00 p.m. Shabbat is over. Eve, Deborah, and David are gathered in the living room, while I'm with Noa in her bedroom. I'm telling her a last story before I go home. Her big eyes devour my face as she savors my whispered words, when suddenly the apartment is pervaded by an awful screaming. It's my daughters: They are shrieking in a way I have never heard before. Cries of horror, their cries so violent you would think their hearts were being torn out. Mine stops. Terrified, Noa bursts into sobs; I clasp her in my arms instinctively, as if to protect her from a nightmare . . . But nothing calms any of them, neither my daughters nor my granddaughter. So I release the child and rush into the living room. Deborah and Eve are still screaming, both of them on the floor in front of David, who is standing there, arms hanging by his sides, not saying a word to stop them. I start screaming, too, although I don't know why. Their eyes are filled with such fear . . . And in the midst of this panic, I realize that my son is absent, that he is the only one who isn't here. I think the worst. I think Ilan's killed himself, Ilan's been in a car accident, he died on the spot. What else?

David moves over to stand beside me; he takes my hands in his. Finally the screaming stops.

"Ilan's been kidnapped."

✦

Kidnapped? It's absurd, but for a second I'm relieved. He's alive when I thought he was dead. Kidnapped. I repeat the word to myself; it means nothing. It's the first time I'm hearing it. Abducted? Kidnapped? Captured? Is that it, David? Is that what you're trying to tell me? I want to ask, but I'm incapable of uttering a sound.

"Mony received a call from a guy who said he was a friend of Ilan's," he continues. "He asked her to connect to the internet and log in to an email address."

"What address?"

"Why?"

"What address? Show me."

"No, Mom. We don't want you to see it," intervenes Eve, holding me by the arm so I can't get to the computer. "They sent a photo. Someone's holding a gun to Ilan's forehead . . ."

✦

I have never seen this image of Ilan seated in front of a large orange sheet, a gun trained on him, his eyes and mouth taped shut, his nose bleeding, and the newspaper *Le Parisien*, showing the date, placed on his knees. My son-in-law and my daughters refused to inflict this torment on me. Later, I discovered the message that accompanied the photo. It was signed Marcel Caron. It had been sent on Saturday, January 21, 2006, at 11:02:41 a.m. The subject line was "LETTER." What it said was this:

> We have ilan and his life is threatened with danger. we demand 450,000 euros [about $550,000 at that time] to release him alive. The transaction will take place on the 23:01:06 morning, i expect your reply to the sender's address before 19h 30 and you will receive the rest of the instructions 22.1.06 before15h. Anything that is consider an obstacles to our actions, we will hold ilan directly responsible.

"Mony told me to meet her in front of your apartment," says David. "We'll go together."

I feel as if I'm hanging off the edge of a cliff, terrified of being sucked into the gaping chasm that, in the space of a few minutes, has opened up beneath us. It's my children who hold me back. They leave me neither time to think nor time to reply. They drag me into the stairwell, and we run downstairs at top speed.

When we reach my building, Mony is already there, waiting.

I have never seen her so pale. In the street she launches into an account of her telephone conversation with the guy who must be the kidnapper. According to her, the man, who seems young—twenty, twenty-five—had a strong African accent. A number had appeared on the screen of her cell phone; she had tried to call back, but obviously no one had picked up. Karim, one of Ilan's best friends, has already done some research. He's discovered that the number in question is that of a phone booth located at 8, place du 25 Août 1944, near the Porte d'Orléans Metro stop. I think one of us suggests going there when Mony's phone begins to ring. We're all paralyzed. Speechless, Mony points to the screen. This time the number is blocked.

"Hello! Hello! So? You have twenty minutes," says a male voice, marked by a strong African accent.

"Wait . . ." stammers Mony, holding her cell phone out to Eve.

My eldest daughter takes the phone, but the guy hangs up before she has time to say a word. I ask for the phone. I want to hold it in my hands, try to call back, do something. But what can I do? And then I see a black man, about thirty years old, walking by our group, staring at us. He stops a few feet away. Not taking his eyes off us, he looks at his cell phone. Exactly as if he were watching us. I've probably gone mad, but the children notice him, too, and Mony, not wanting to be overheard, whispers in my ear: "They have the keys to our apartments . . . yours and mine. I saw Ilan's key chain in the photo . . ."

The man walks back toward us. What does he want from us? I try to memorize his features and his build. He's young, tall, well-built; he's wearing a pair of black trousers and a zip-up pullover. Short hair, no glasses, no mustache. No distinguishing features. I'm sure his presence here is no coincidence as, this evening, nothing can be. But how can we be sure? I'll never know if this guy was one of the criminals or just a simple passerby who was intrigued at seeing us in such a state of panic . . .

"We have to inform your father," I say to my daughters.

This isn't something they've heard me say often. Didier and I have been divorced for twenty years, and we haven't been in touch for ages. He lives in Paris. The children see him, but I never do. This evening, though, I need him.

David calls the children's father. He tells him about the photo and the message we received by email. From the silence that follows, we understand that Didier is digesting the information. Like me, he's incapable of uttering a word. David continues the conversation. He asks Didier if he's received any unusual calls. Yes, there had been about ten on his cell phone, but since they were from an unknown number, he hadn't answered.

"What was the number?" David asks him. When he gives David the number, David replies, "It's the phone booth."

"What phone booth?" asks Didier.

"A phone booth near Porte d'Orléans—we checked. That's where the kidnapper called Mony from the first time. It looks as if he tried to contact you, too."

"Where are you now?"

"On the street in front of Ruth's place."

"Let's meet now at the police station closest to her."

While we're on our way, the man calls Mony again. It's the third time. Again, we hang on his every word. However, nothing he says is reassuring. He just asks questions that he repeats over and over again. "Are you going to pay? Do you agree? Do you have the money? You're going to pay? Are you going to pay?" Mony manages to reply. She promises he'll get everything he wants, but she begs him not to hurt Ilan. She asks to speak to Ilan. The guy refuses. He says he'll contact her tomorrow with instructions, and the money has to be handed over on Monday—two days from now.

My daughters encircle me, each holding one of my hands tightly. They're worried that the shock will be too much for me. And they talk and talk. They don't stop talking . . . They are numbed by the flow of words they utter to control their panic, but they also keep repeating the same thing: "Don't worry, Mom. We'll pay. How much do they want—450,000 euros? We'll find it. We'll find a solution. Don't worry." It's like being in a bad movie; they've gone mad . . .

When we reach the police station, Didier is waiting for us at the door with Ilan's two best friends, Karim and Jérémie. I have no idea who told them to meet us here. All of us can't go in—there's no point. So we decide it will be Jérémie, Karim, and Mony, escorted by Didier. They're the ones Ilan confides in the most. I wait outside with my two daughters. A quarter of an hour, half an hour, one hour . . . Their statements are never-ending. They answer the usual questions the police ask: "When did you last see Ilan?" "Did he seem worried lately?" "Did he have money problems? Debts?" "Did he keep bad company?"

Out on the street, we ask ourselves the same questions: What has Ilan gotten himself into? Whom had he gone out with last night? Who would wish him ill? Tell us, God, who could have done something like this? But no, it's just a bad joke. Any other hypothesis is unthinkable.

✦

After a meeting that lasts two hours, Ilan's friends and my ex-husband emerge. They tell us we've come to the wrong place. This local police station says they can't help us. We have to go to the central police station on boulevard Louis-Blanc, in the Tenth Arrondissement. That's where the Third District Criminal

Investigation Bureau is located. They're used to handling serious crimes; they'll be able to help us. So the police consider it a serious case. They don't think it's a joke, or that he's run away. I would so much have liked to believe that, just for a short while longer . . .

At boulevard Louis-Blanc, we go over our story once again. The first call, to Mony's cell phone at about 7:00 this evening; a man with an African accent who asks her to connect to an email account and gives her a password to do so; the message she finds when she does; 450,000 euros' ransom if she wants to see Ilan alive again; his photo as an attachment, a gun held to his forehead, his nose bleeding, his eyes and mouth taped shut. The police officers take note, but at midnight they, in turn, admit that our case is beyond their scope, and they send us to the regional headquarters of the Police Judiciaire (PJ), the French equivalent of the FBI, located at 36, quai des Orfèvres. The address of the PJ leaves us speechless. We've all heard it in films. It's synonymous with murder, organized crime, drug trafficking, and terrorism. What have we gotten ourselves into?

March 10, 2015

LOS ANGELES—UCLA sophomore Rachel Beyda seemed like a shoo-in for a spot on the student council's prestigious Judicial Board, which acts as the Supreme Court for the UCLA student body. But when the economics major and aspiring attorney arrived at her confirmation hearing on February 10, she was confronted by a string of ugly insinuations and questions from fellow students about whether her Judaism and her involvement in Jewish campus groups would affect her ability to be objective. After a heated exchange, the Undergraduate Students Association Council voted to reject her nomination. Beyda eventually won a spot on the board after a second vote held later that night. In the wake of Beyda's confirmation hearing, the UCLA Undergraduate Students Association Council passed a resolution condemning anti-Semitism by a vote of 12–0. But as Avinoam Baral, who nominated Beyda, told the *New York Times,* "It's very problematic to me that students would feel it was appropriate to ask those kinds of questions...." He added that, "We've been questioned all of our history: Are Jews loyal citizens? Don't they have divided loyalties? All of these anti-Semitic tropes."

Day 2

The Investigation Gets Underway

36, Quai des Orfèvres

"It's already midnight. You don't have to wait outside again in the cold," my children tell me, urging me to go in. "If there's any news, we'll call."

I agree. I'm like a little girl, overwhelmed by anxiety, paralyzed, incapable of taking the slightest initiative. So David and my girls drop me at home before going off to the Île de la Cité. There, they meet detectives from the Anti-Crime Brigade, the unit that's in charge of "kidnappings for ransom."

Once again, the detectives at 36, quai des Orfèvres take their statements, read the email, look at the photo of Ilan, and bombard them with questions. They're trying to understand why a young man like my son was abducted. If the kidnapper chose him, there must be a reason. But what is it? No one in the family has the means to pay 450,000 euros. Ilan is a salesman at a cell-phone store; he earns 1,200 euros a month. My eldest child, Eve, is looking for a job. Deborah, the youngest, is an assistant at a consulting company. And my son-in-law works at a real estate agency. As for me, I'm a secretary, and Didier, my ex-husband, owns a store. We don't fit the typical profile of people worth holding up for ransom. So what's going on? Does it have something to do with a gambling debt or a drug deal? No, the investigators soon agree that Ilan is an ordinary young man. The only "interesting" thing they notice is that, at the beginning of the week, Ilan had met a charming female client at his place of work. Yesterday, Friday, he was to meet her at a café at Porte d'Orléans. Porte d'Orléans? The phone booth the kidnapper had called us from is also at Porte d'Orléans. My son had told Jérémie about the meeting, but, unfortunately, that's all he knows about it. As for Mony, obviously she has no idea . . .

At four o'clock in the morning, today, Sunday, January 22, the Anti-Crime Brigade finally tells Didier and the children they can leave, promising to do everything possible to identify the girl. She's our only lead. The detectives think she was used as a lure in Ilan's kidnapping, but they know nothing at all about her. Nor do my girls, and they can't resign themselves to going home to sleep. Until daybreak, they drive around the Porte d'Orléans. If only they could find their brother's Renault Twingo . . .

The Trap

Why did this girl choose my son? When and where did she first decide to target him? Was it a long time ago—in a bar, in the street, or looking through the store window? Did she go into the store because he was alone, and there were no customers? Did she pretend that she was interested in buying a phone? Did she play her part so convincingly that she let him describe all the features of the latest cell phone? Or did she simply ask him for his number? In any event, she got it and called him back. Told him she wanted to see him again on Friday evening, at a café at Porte d'Orléans.

At dawn this morning, when Eve got back from the Quai des Orfèvres, she told me about this "amorous" meeting, and since then I can't help trying to imagine the girl, seated opposite my son, promising him so much . . .

Later, I discover that this mystery girl suggested they go back to her place for a drink. I learn that they parked in a parking lot not far from Jean Monnet University in Sceaux. They walked down the "green alley" that runs alongside the university building, and, in this silent, desolate spot, she said the word key, which was the signal for two hooded men, hiding in the bushes, to jump out and grab my son.

The following day, Saturday, some of the local residents informed the police that they had heard piercing screams in the night. The cries were so high-pitched they thought a woman was being attacked. Why didn't they call the police immediately? Why did they wait until the next morning? Why didn't anyone open a window? Now I have to live with all these whys . . .

Eventually, once the police have her in custody, the lure says that Ilan shrieked "like a girl," but it didn't bother her for long. Once her "mission" was over, at one in the morning, an accomplice calmly drove her back to Paris. He dropped her in the vicinity of Montparnasse, where she went to dinner with a young man she had met on the internet. That night, they took a room at a Hotel Formule 1, where she paid with the money she had earned by enticing Ilan into a trap. And—the perfect ending to a wonderful evening—they made love, and she later found herself pregnant. I wonder, did she think of Ilan when she woke up the next morning? Did she think of his suffering? Of ours?

For my part, I think of her. All the time. Constantly. I think of this girl who seduced my son, knowing he was going to be locked away. In my dreams I beg her. If she had just made one phone call, even anonymously, it would have been over. I ask her to feel remorse for what she did, to have pity on him, to give me back my child. For three interminable weeks, she is my strongest hope.

A Game of Cat and Mouse

Today, Sunday, the kidnapper calls Mony again in the morning. First he sends her a text message to say the ransom has to be paid in installments, with a first payment of 100,000 euros. Half an hour later he reiterates his demands, but this time he speaks to her from a phone booth in Gentilly, just outside Paris.

Officers of the Forensic Identification Service go to the phone booth there immediately but find no clues that can help them in the investigation. The man who made the call had undoubtedly worn gloves. As for the phone number he used to send the text message, the detectives are unable to track it down. The user has probably switched off the phone and removed the battery. I learn that it's impossible to trace a cell phone that doesn't have a battery.

We don't have the 100,000 euros he wants as a first installment. We know nobody who could lend us so much money, and the police won't pay. They don't give in to blackmail. Maybe they're planning to hand over a stack of counterfeit notes? I don't know. I don't know anything. I'm all alone at home and keep going around in circles like a goldfish in a bowl. I try to keep my hopes up by thinking of tomorrow. The transaction will take place tomorrow morning—"The transaction will take place on the 23:01:06 morning"—that's what the kidnapper wrote in his email.

In the early afternoon, two detectives from the Anti-Crime Brigade ring my doorbell. They want to have a look at Ilan's belongings. I let them in, of course. I allow them to rummage through our private lives, and it's unbearable. They open Ilan's closets, examine his clothes, his papers, his writing on the sticky notes scribbled in haste, as if each detail could tell us where he is . . . The sight of our lives laid out on display, handed over to them, terrifies me. It's proof that I no longer have control over anything.

The police officers take Ilan's computer and tell me to come to the Quai des Orfèvres. Why do I need to go there? Why do I have to leave everything up to them? Am I no longer capable of managing anything on my own? Yes, I brought up my three children single-handedly. Yes, I brought them up and protected them by myself. I was strong enough to do that. Why do I now need these men? I feel so helpless . . .

Outside, the streets smell of Sunday. As I drive, I notice that there's little traffic, metal shutters are lowered, families are out for walks . . . My eyes register a few random snapshots: a kid on a bicycle; a woman with a tired smile, begging at the traffic light; the silhouettes of the other drivers who stop next to me . . . Life goes by outside my car window like a speeded-up film. I feel as if I'm no longer a part of it. My forehead bangs against the window, my fingers slip down it, and I wonder if I'll ever have the opportunity to be part of this world again . . .

I've never been to 36, quai des Orfèvres, and the first thing that jumps out at me, *that makes my blood run cold*, is the wall covered in photos of missing people. There are dozens of faces: children, adolescents, adults—so many lives, and no one knows what has become of them. Behind the pictures, how many broken families?

Not knowing is torture. Knowing is too, very often. Wondering interminably, every second: Is my child suffering? Did he suffer? How can you not go mad? I turn away; I try to erase these images from my mind, but they'll never leave me.

On the fourth floor, a woman takes my statement. She tries to understand the kind of family we are, who Ilan is, what he likes, how he spends his time. She cannot accept that he was a plain-dealing sort of boy. So I have to keep repeating it. Hammering it home. But this policewoman persists. "I'm sure you don't know everything about his life," she says to me. "Are you sure he isn't on drugs?"

Although she's only doing her job, her questions nag at me like suspicions. And they sully Ilan, forcing me to defend him as if he were likely to be held responsible for what's happening to him. The absurdity of this situation petrifies me. Will I have to fight the police, too?

And while we try to understand—just understand—how my son could have been kidnapped in the heart of Paris, in another office Mony and Didier are looking at the electronic mailbox to which the first message was sent. The kidnappers—the police believe there is more than one—have just sent another message, but this time from a different address. Their email is signed FABRICEGUIOP. It says:

> meeting on 23.01.2006 at chatelet les halles, in front of k f c at exactly 08h 00. you have to have a cell phone, a computer connected to the Internet. You have to bring 10 people with their identity cards to the meeting point. And I will send you the rest of the information for the first part of the ransom at that time.

The chief inspector realizes immediately what the kidnappers are up to. If they're asking for a computer with a Wi-Fi connection, they're probably planning to ask for a virtual payment, a bank transfer, which would make the usual outcome in these situations impossible: a briefcase filled with money in exchange for the hostage. To make sure, the chief inspector asks Mony to send a naive-sounding reply to the text message she had received in the morning about paying in installments. He dictates what she is to say:

> Received message from Fabrice Guiop. Why 10 people at KFC? Don't have laptop with Internet. Call me back.

Then the chief inspector sends one of his police officers to a cybercafe with Mony. She has to email the following message to Marcel Caron's address and to Fabrice Guiop's address:

> I've received your instructions. I don't have a laptop computer connected to the Internet. What should I do? I don't know ten people who could come with me tomorrow morning. Should I tell people? I'm worried about Ilan, I want to hear from him. Thanks.

✦

The chief inspector hopes the kidnappers will reply immediately, but they don't respond. Their silence is terribly disturbing. The police are well aware that in kidnapping cases the first hours are decisive. Ilan was kidnapped late Friday night or early Saturday morning, and it's already Sunday afternoon. As time passes, the chances of finding him decrease. At 9:00 p.m., the chief inspector orders Mony to send the kidnappers a second text message, as well as another email. She writes:

> I'm worried, I haven't heard from you. I've sent you text messages and emails and you haven't replied. What do you want me to do? I don't have the money yet and I don't know where to find such a large sum on a Sunday. As I said, I don't have a laptop computer with an Internet connection. What should I do? Please, please reply and send me some news of Ilan. Tell me he's okay, I want to talk to him.

The kidnappers have stopped responding. They've broken off all contact. We don't even know if Ilan is still alive. What else have they done to him since the photograph they sent us yesterday? Have they beaten him again? In the photo, his nose was bloody. Have they pressed the trigger of the gun? No, they couldn't have; that would leave them with no means of forcing us to pay the ransom. But why the silence? What are they going to do? Have they abandoned their plans? Has my son managed to escape?

I know nothing, only that the ransom won't be handed over tomorrow morning as initially planned. The first meeting set up by the kidnappers has effectively been canceled as we have no further instructions. So Ilan's ordeal will continue.

For how much longer?

February 25, 2018

CHICAGO—Nation of Islam leader Louis Farrakhan continued his decades-long legacy of anti-Semitic attacks during his annual Saviours' Day speech in Chicago, telling followers that Jews were responsible for the 9/11 attacks and referring to Judaism as "the Synagogue of Satan." He also revived long-standing lies about Jewish control of the US government—a favorite refrain among white supremacists. There was almost no public criticism of Farrakhan's overt anti-Semitism, prompting the *Forward's* Ben Faulding, who is black and Jewish, to write, "Louis Farrakhan is more than just a bigot, a homophobe, a misogynist or an anti-Semite. ... He is an exploiter.... No civilized discourse or progress can move forward with him, or anyone who associates with him."

Day 3

Tracing the Kidnappers' Blueprint

The Lure's Trail

FROM TELEPHONE RECORDS, the Anti-Crime Brigade manages to retrace Ilan's movements on Friday evening. After leaving the house at about 9:30 p.m., my son called several of his close friends—Karim, Jérémie, and Mony. Then he went to the Nineteenth Arrondissement, where another one of his friends lives. At around 11:00 p.m., he received a call from the phone booth at Porte d'Orléans—the one the kidnapper used to contact us the first time. It was most likely the lure. They must have planned to meet at a café nearby, since the conversation only lasted a few seconds, and Ilan went straight to the Fourteenth Arrondissement, as his mobile location tracker shows. His phone pinged for the last time on Saturday, at 12:45 a.m., in a suburb of Sceaux, not far from Jean Monnet University. After that, there is no electronic trace of Ilan. The criminals must have made sure his phone was switched off and the battery removed, which is what they're doing with all the phones they're using.

The list of calls my son received during the week before his abduction, which the Anti-Crime Brigade obtained from the telephone company, provides other information. Among the numbers listed, the investigators recognize the one from which the text message was sent to Mony on Sunday morning. This number belongs to a man named Jules Huet. The police have no difficulty finding him, but after several checks, it turns out that he has nothing to do with any of these events: He's just had his phone stolen.

In order to identify the fraudulent user, investigators examine all calls sent from Huet's line since it was stolen. Apart from Ilan, only one other person has been called: Maurice Keller. He is also a salesperson at a cell-phone store on boulevard Voltaire.

This is it—the police have found the culprit! They assume that my son's kidnapping has something to do with a cell-phone racket and that this Keller is most probably the person behind the abduction. They prepare to arrest him without further ado.

Two plainclothes policemen tail Keller in a car as he leaves his place of work. They take advantage of a red light to confront him. Keller is instructed to exit his vehicle and to place his hands on his head. He is handcuffed, then taken directly to the Anti-Crime Brigade.

"We have a few questions for you regarding an investigation into the kidnapping and holding of the person called Ilan Halimi," says the law enforcement officer who questions him. "Do you know him?"

"No, I don't know him," replies Keller. "I've never seen him," he states, studying the photo they hold out in front of him. Keller is trembling, and he has difficulty controlling his voice:

"I know what's happened—my colleague told me about it. She told me her friend Eve's brother's been kidnapped, and he works at a cell-phone store like me. That's all I know."

"Do you know this phone number?" the officer asks, showing him Huet's number?

"No," Keller replies.

The officer who had confiscated Keller's phone runs through his address book. And he finds Huet's number. It's saved under a first name with no surname, Lea.

"Who's Lea?"

"I don't know her," Keller tells them. "She's a girl I hardly saw. She came into my store two Saturdays ago. I was busy with a client, so she spoke to my brother, who works with me. She said to him, 'I haven't come to buy a phone. I just want the other salesman's phone number, since I'd like to go out with him.' My brother gave her my number, and she left me a message that very evening. Then she sent a very tantalizing text message. I tried to call her back but couldn't get through. I spoke to her on Monday or Tuesday. She wanted us to go out for a drink. I found her strange, so I refused. I never heard from her again after that."

✦

What if Keller had agreed? And if he'd had a drink with her? Would he be in Ilan's position now, handcuffed, gagged, a gun to his forehead? Having started out suspecting Keller, the police begin to realize that he was a prospective victim, not one of the kidnappers. Would that mean my son was kidnapped at random? They chose him, but could they just as easily have chosen Keller? Who was the kidnappers' real target? A phone salesman? A store owner on boulevard Voltaire? Did they think these two were rich enough to be able to pay a ransom of 450,000 euros? It seems highly unlikely . . . So why Keller? Why Ilan? What do they have in common? Nothing other than their youth, and their profession . . . Oh, yes, and something else: They're both Jewish.

✦

"What else do you know about this girl?" asks the officer.

"She told me that she was twenty-four, that she was a beautician in Paris, and that she lived in Sceaux."

Keller remembers that she mentioned Sceaux because he had thought to himself that it was quite a distance away. The name of the suburb alerts the detectives, too, as Ilan's cell phone had last been pinging in that area, shortly after midnight, the night he was kidnapped.

"What does she look like?"

"She's pretty, well put together. I'd say she's about twenty. She has long hair, very blond, a bit wavy. She must be about five foot four."

"Anything distinctive—jewelry, glasses?"

"No. She was wearing a very tight, white T-shirt—she had impressive breasts—and a long black coat."

Did Lea move on to Ilan after having tried to seduce Keller? It sounds obvious enough, but the statement made by Gabriel Petit, a salesman who works at the store opposite Ilan's, seems to contradict this hypothesis. On Tuesday, January 17, at about 5:00 p.m., Petit received a call from my son asking him to take a look at the girl who was leaving his shop. Ilan had just been approached by her in a flirtatious way, and he wanted his friend's opinion. So Petit moved over to the window and saw a North African–looking brunette. "Not bad," he said to Ilan. "Attractive."

“I gave her my number. She said she’d call me,” my son replied.

Keller’s description of Lea doesn’t match the girl Petit saw—Keller saw a blond, Petit a brunette. But their direct pickup lines, and the fact that they both used Huet’s stolen phone—the same one the kidnappers are using—leaves the investigators in no doubt that both these girls are lures, working for the group that has seized Ilan.

The detectives at 36, quai des Orfèvres immediately have forensic sketch artists make drawings of Lea and the brunette. I imagine they’re going to plaster these sketches all over France, put them up in police stations, bakeries, the Metro . . . Once again I’m filled with hope, convinced that someone, somewhere, will recognize them. But my hopes are soon dashed. The Quai des Orfèvres decides not to broadcast anything. They believe this may endanger Ilan’s life. And I have to trust them.

Communications Resume

Mony spends Sunday night at my home. We don’t sleep. We are glued to our cell phones, checking every few minutes that our network is working. It’s only at eight o’clock in the morning that Mony’s cell finally rings. I think our hearts will stop.

“Is everything ready? You have the cash? You have the money?” asks the same voice Mony heard the previous day.

“I’m worried about Ilan,” replies Mony. “How is he? Where is he? I want to speak to him. Please, I beg you, tell me how he is!”

“Listen! I’m telling you, listen to me!” shouts the man.

I can hear him out in the corridor where I’m standing. The tone of his voice is enough to paralyze me.

“You got the money?” he repeats.

"No, I don't," admits Mony. "The banks are closed on Sundays."

"Ah, okay. Yesterday you said yes, so you're messing around with me . . . You're playing with his life . . ."

There's a sadistic tone to his voice that would make anyone crumple, but Mony stands her ground.

"Tell me how he is."

"You don't think I'm serious, is that it? Answer me. All I have to do is make one phone call, and that's it. It's all over for him."

"I'm begging you, just tell me . . ."

"The police are listening, I know."

"No, there's no one here, I just want to know how he is."

"I'm in charge, you fucking slut! I'll send you a photo of him with his face bashed in. We're going to torture him a bit, you'll see. How much do you have?"

"Don't hurt him, please . . ."

"How much do you have? I'm asking you."

"Is he still alive?"

The man is silent. For a second, maybe two, but it seems like an eternity.

"He's fine," he whispers before hanging up.

The conversation lasts just a few minutes. In a panic, Mony immediately calls back the number displayed on the screen of her cell. It's not "Lea's," or the phone booths at Porte d'Orléans or Porte-de-Gentilly, which we now know by heart. It's a foreign number, starting with 225. No one answers.

"He's okay," Mony keeps repeating like a mantra, as if she doesn't believe it herself. Her eyes fill with tears. So do mine, and we both cry for a long time in the silence of his absence. We've been holding back our tears for so long . . .

The Quai des Orfèvres Strategy

After hanging up on Mony, the kidnapper contacts my ex-husband. The kidnapper complains that "The girl isn't up to it." He wants to know whether he, Didier, has managed to get the money together. The kidnapper suggests a compromise: 50,000 euros this morning; 50,000 euros tomorrow, Tuesday.

It's an odd proposition, since the kidnapper doesn't mention the remaining 350,000 euros to make up his initial ransom demand, or the way it's to be handed over. Didier asks him what to do, but the conversation is interrupted.

The man calls back a few seconds later, saying he just wants to avoid having the call traced. He asks whether the police have been informed.

Didier replies that they haven't, of course not, and, strangely, the kidnapper says he's out of the country. Didier doesn't follow this up. He claims he needs time to pull together the money.

The kidnapper goes berserk: "You're not the one in charge here, I'm the one running this show."

He hangs up again and calls back a third time. He now seems overexcited, less sure of himself . . . as if suddenly he doesn't know what to do next. It makes him aggressive. Just as he had said to Mony, he promises to send Didier a photo of Ilan, with his "head bashed in."

✦

The Quai des Orfèvres has been informed about these calls. The Anti-Crime Brigade asks Mony and Didier to come down to their offices immediately. I'd like to go, too, but I'm kept out of it. The detectives think I won't be able to stay calm. They're worried about what I might say. Or do. So they decide that

Didier will be the only one to speak to the kidnappers. I can do nothing but agree.

But, as it turns out, Didier is to have no more freedom than I will. He will only be an intermediary. From now on, everything he says to our son's captors is to be dictated to him by a psychologist and two hostage negotiators.

The Choice of a Jew

Over the course of this Monday morning the kidnapper calls numerous times, and, from his voice, the detectives deduce that the man is between twenty and thirty years old. From his accent they believe he is of African descent. This hypothesis is all the more likely as the foreign number he calls from is a cell phone that's being used on an Ivory Coast network. It's what's known as a "publiphone" in Africa, a cell phone that clients can pay to use. Which makes it impossible to identify the criminal.

Although investigators note that most of his linguistic expressions reflect standard suburban French usage, they don't think they're dealing with a hoodlum from the *cités,* the low-income social housing projects. They're convinced that the kidnapper is in Ivory Coast and that he knows perfectly well how telephone and internet networks function. They see him as the leader of a criminal network in Africa that has branches in France. They don't for an instant believe that the guy who's been leading them on this fool's errand for the last forty-eight hours is a small-time delinquent from Bagneux, whose sketch is thumbtacked to the walls of police stations throughout the Paris area. How could they imagine that this twenty-five-year-old kid is so cocky that he's off vacationing in his parents' country while his pals at Pierre-

Plate, an enormous housing project in the town of Bagneux, are guarding the hostage?

✦

Since Didier and Mony can't leave the Quai des Orfèvres and risk missing a call, at about 1:00 p.m. my son-in-law David takes them some sandwiches. The three of them have lunch there with the Anti-Gang Brigade negotiators, in a small room that's been transformed into a wiretap room. Suddenly Didier's cell phone rings. One of the policemen switches on the tape recorder, and my ex-husband answers.

At the other end of the line, a man is singing.

For about a minute, he sings, or rather chants, words he seems to know by heart, in a foreign language, without a break.

He doesn't speak, he doesn't demand anything.

He just sings.

He sings in Arabic.

"Did you hear?" asks Didier, once the call has ended.

"What was he saying?" asks David.

A policeman of North African descent replies, "It's Arabic. He was reading a passage from the Koran."

Didier, David, and Mony break down. They all immediately think of the photo of Ilan we received. Handcuffed, tied up, gagged. They see this unbearable image, and their minds conjure up another series of images—of our journalists who are being held hostage by Muslim fundamentalists. . . How can they help but make the connection?

The kidnapper is calling from Africa. Could Ilan be a prisoner in a house in a suburb of Abidjan in Ivory Coast? Could religious fanatics have seized him? But why did they choose Ilan of all people? In Paris? Until now, they've spoken of nothing but money. Are they now going to say they're affiliated with a political or religious cause?

As promised, the kidnapper calls back. This time he speaks French. He is no longer singing. He goes over the instructions he gave Didier that very morning, concerning a first installment of 50,000 euros. Now, he says it's not enough and he goes back to demanding 450,000 euros.

Didier repeats what the negotiators whisper to him: "I don't have that amount."

"You'll just have to ask the Jewish community," retorts the man, before he breaks the connection.

The Jewish community? What does the Jewish community have to do with any of this? And how does the kidnapper know we're Jewish anyway? We aren't Orthodox Jews; nothing in our appearance reveals the religion we belong to. Ilan doesn't wear a *kippah* or any other external sign of religious belief. When they kidnapped him, he was wearing faded jeans, a pair of sneakers, and a leather jacket. Just like any other boy his age!

The kidnapper knows Ilan is Jewish because he specifically chose a Jew. I'm convinced of it the moment David and Mony tell me about their day at the Quai des Orfèvres. And I'm certain because the other boy, the one who might have been kidnapped instead of Ilan, is also Jewish. They weren't looking to kidnap a cell-phone salesman—what would be the point? They were looking for a Jew. Any young Jewish man, whether he worked at a cell-phone store or not, was a potential target. Otherwise why would the kidnapper now be suggesting we ask the Jewish community for help?

The chief inspector, with whom I share my conclusions, thinks I'm mistaken. The kidnapper recites the Koran. He mentions the Jewish community; Maurice Keller, who narrowly avoided the trap is Jewish, too, and the chief inspector says I'm on the wrong track? Why is he refusing to see what's really going on here? Why won't he see the reality that's staring him in the face? Why is he being so obstinate when he knows Ilan isn't the first Jew to have crossed the path of a thug of this caliber? It had happened to several doctors, then to Martin Durand.

✦

At the beginning of 2005, several Jewish doctors had lodged complaints with the police about blackmail. Bogus patients would go to their clinics and have the doctor prescribe a few days off work, although they weren't really ill. The people all claimed to live on rue Serge Prokofiev in Bagneux, the very street on which Ilan would be imprisoned and tortured. So the investigators knew this address; it was spelled out in all the doctors' files. Had the police ever even gone there?

The racketeers would call the doctors back a few days later, threatening to denounce them to the medical board if they didn't pay extortion money. Just as in our case, the negotiations took place using two email addresses created especially for this purpose. The same distinctive method hadn't escaped the detectives' notice. Right at the beginning of the investigation, they suspected that the same extortionists were at work again, but this time they'd moved up a level to taking hostages. Investigators immediately recognized that this wasn't the kidnappers' first attempt: Another Jew, Martin Durand, had, by the skin of his teeth, just escaped a kidnapping attempt on January 6, 2006, in Arcueil. Barely two weeks before Ilan disappeared.

Durand's near-disaster began at the beginning of December, while he was at home with his adult son, Jacques. A "singer," called Melvina, suddenly turned up on their doorstep. This young lady wanted to make it in the music world, and she claimed she had heard that Jacques was a record producer, so that's why she had decided to knock on his door. Jacques responded that he no longer worked in that field so he couldn't do anything for her, but she kept insisting until he finally agreed to give her his phone number. From then on, Melvina harassed him with phone calls. She finally got him to agree to a meeting on January 5.

Jacques gave in to get rid of her, but he didn't show up. Although she realized that she had been stood up, Melvina didn't give up. On the contrary: At 10:00 p.m. on January 5, 2006, she turned up unexpectedly on his doorstep again. Frederic Arnaud, a friend who was staying with Martin Durand at the time, let her in. Durand immediately called Jacques to inform him. Exasperated, the ex-producer asked Arnaud to get rid of this "annoying girl" and to tell her he would not be back that night. Arnaud politely asked Melvina to leave.

But an hour later, the singer was back, prepared to wait as long as needed for Jacques. This time, Arnaud was moved by her story: He told her to wait in the living room.

Around midnight, Martin Durand returned to find his friend deep in conversation with the pretty young woman. Durand also treated her in a friendly manner and then offered to drive her home, since it was so late. According to Durand's account, he dropped Melvina off in front of a building in Arcueil. Then the so-called singer demanded that he accompany her to the building's entrance, claiming that she did not feel safe. Durand had no objection, until he realized that she was trying to draw him into the stairwell leading to the basement.

"Is this really where you live?" he asked her.

Caught off guard, Melvina improvised. She said she wanted to take him to a space where she usually rehearsed, to pick up some demos for him to give to his son. Then she claimed that she had lost her keys, she had to go to her mother's, and she would be back right away. She disappeared, abandoning Durand in the hallway for five minutes. When she returned, she asked him to drop her at Bagneux, at a girlfriend's place. Durand agreed, without asking any questions.

That should have been the end of it, but, early the next evening, Melvina called Durand. She kept telling him how much she dreamed of a career in the music world, and she begged him to arrange a meeting with his son. Durand told her again that his son had changed careers, and he really couldn't help her. But Melvina appeared to be so upset that when she suggested they meet at the Arcueil train station, he didn't know how to refuse. And to cheer her up, he took her out to dinner at a bistro in Saint-Germain-des-Prés. Then, as he had the previous night, he dropped her at home, accompanying her into the hall of the building in Arcueil. Less cautious this time, he followed her into the stairwell leading to the basement. A bad decision. Two men hit him on the head, and he lost consciousness immediately. Having heard his cries, some tenants rushed to the basement. They found Durand lying on the ground, his face covered in blood, his ankles and wrists handcuffed.

✦

On January 6, Martin Durand lodged a complaint with the police. The investigation into this blatant assault case would be terminated on January 20—the day Ilan is kidnapped—and in a few days it would be transferred to the regional court in Créteil. The committing magistrate at this court would send a letter of request to Criminal Investigation Department 94. Then, in early February, he would hand the case over to the investigating judge in Paris in charge of Ilan's kidnapping. In turn, the judge would send a letter of request to the Anti-Crime Brigade, authorizing them to carry out a parallel investigation into the attack on Martin Durand, on the premise that the people who attacked him are the same as those who kidnapped my son.

✦

The police quickly made a connection between these very similar methods: the presence of a lure, negotiations using email addresses specially created for this purpose, as well as the geographical proximity of the attacks—Arcueil and Bagneux in Durand's case, Sceaux in Ilan's. But the most important common denominator in all these different cases seems to have escaped the investigators. They never noticed that all the victims were Jewish. The doctors who were blackmailed, Maurice Keller, Martin and Jacques Durand, and Ilan. How could anyone imagine that in 2006, in France, the life of a Jew could still be at risk, just because he was Jewish?

On Tuesday, January 17, 2006, the man we presumed was the ringleader had taken his lure to boulevard Voltaire, pointing out the cell-phone shops, which he described as belonging to Jews. "He knew they were," the girl would later say, because he had noticed that on Saturdays, Shabbat, a lot of the shops in the Sentier neighborhood and on boulevard Voltaire were closed. And he wanted to kidnap a Jew because, according to him, "Jews are rich, they belong to a very close-knit community that's willing to pay." Mere prejudice, said some. How could they have dismissed the gravity of his words like that?

Like millions of Jews before him, my son died because of this prejudice. Anyone with a memory knows full well that anti-Semitism is founded on this fallacy. The myth of the Jew and his money was the main theme of Nazi propaganda, the leitmotif of the fascist press and radio programs, the delusion the collaborators who shamelessly sent their compatriots to their deaths labored under. But today, some say that those who shouted, "The Jew will pay, he can pay," were nothing like the hoodlums from Bagneux. They claim they were anti-Semitic because they had a certain culture, as if anti-Semitism were a question of culture, as if the SS militias had never recruited people from the underworld . . . Does this mean that, because they come from underprivileged backgrounds, my son's torturers are incapable of hating Jews? That they can't be anti-Semitic, as the federal prosecutor would explain, because they're among "the lowest of the low in terms of their ability to think"? But it seems to me that hatred has never had anything to do with intelligence. On the contrary, hatred is a gut reaction, and what kind of hatred motivated these young people to hold Ilan prisoner for three weeks, to starve him, torture him, beat him, burn him, and finally abandon him like a dog in the woods? Boundless hatred. An absolute hatred of Jews, whom the presumed ringleader of the gang claimed were "kings." As later quoted in the newspaper *Le Monde*, "He believed, the lure remembers, that Jews devoured the State's money, and as he was black, the State saw him as a slave."

This fantasy—of Jewish control of the banks, of the economy—that I once heard a stand-up comedian use in a show, has made its way into popular thought . . . It's rotted these young gang members' brains enough to turn them into barbarians. There are words that kill. And images, too. Footage of militant Islamists spewing their anti-Semitic hatred on satellite channels—how can no one realize they influenced Ilan's kidnappers? How could no one see that this man, who chanted a passage from the Koran over the telephone and then asked us to call upon the Jewish community, was driven by the same hatred for the Jews as these religious fanatics?

Anyone who still has any doubts should have seen my son's killer on October 17, 2007, in front of the Sixteenth Paris District Criminal Court. While awaiting trial for Ilan's murder, he was appearing in court for "outrage to a magistrate," after having sent an insulting letter to the judge, accompanied by a photo of a Palestinian suicide bomber who had blown himself up in a discotheque in Tel Aviv. Wearing a white cap, Youssouf Fofana—who will turn out to be the mastermind behind Ilan's kidnapping and murder—got up and cried out: "In the name of the Muslims and Africans who are the victims of Zionist terrorists, bearded men wearing *kippahs, inshallah,* a commando will come to release me."

For that, he was sentenced to a year in prison; he greeted the sentence with a cry of "*Allah Akbar*" (God is great).

Day 4

Disarray in the Police Force

"Tell me you'll find him."

"We're doing everything we can, Madam."

"You can't not find him, it's impossible, isn't it? Promise me you'll bring Ilan back . . ."

I implore the two policemen who sleep in my drawing room, just as I am to plead with many more of them over the next weeks. Today, the Quai des Orfèvres decided that Didier and I should have police protection at night. So every evening, each of us sees a range of staff from the Anti-Crime, Anti-Gang, and Anti-Drug Brigades, and the organized crime division parade through our respective apartments.

The two men who are here on this first evening assure me that the police are doing everything they possibly can. They've deployed all the means at their disposal to find Ilan. Everyone at 36, quai des Orfèvres, they say, is working on the case. And to convince me, they assure me that everything else is on hold, as all the other cases are felonies. Unlike Ilan, the victims are no longer alive. I have the clear feeling that our story is theirs, too, the kind of event that marks a policeman's career, and failure would be difficult to bear. But, despite all their goodwill and their energy, I also feel they're unprepared for this kind of situation. The last person who was kidnapped in France was Baron Empain, in January 1978. Are young officers still trained to deal with cases like this? Do they have any idea what kidnappers' profiles are like? The way they operate? Hasn't it changed over thirty years anyway? Baron Empain was eventually released, but I remember that his kidnappers had cut off one of his fingers to send to the family. The policemen haven't forgotten that either, and they don't know what to say to me.

"Don't worry," one of them finally says. "They don't kidnap people to kill them. They won't kill your son."

✦

Nonetheless, the police wonder whether Ilan is still alive. Given the kidnapper's irritability, they have serious doubts. Today the kidnapper called Didier more than twenty times. He's still asking for the ransom, but the amount keeps changing: It goes from 25,000 to 450,000 euros in less than a quarter of an hour. And when Ilan's father offers to make a payment of 110,000 euros, the kidnapper doesn't know what to say and hangs up. Calls. Hangs up. Gets irritated, threatens, sets up a new meeting at the KFC in Les Halles. Now Didier is supposed to go there accompanied by three people, rather than ten, but he still needs a laptop computer. Which day, what time? The kidnapper probably doesn't know himself.

The kidnapper's in such a panic that, by the end of the afternoon, the investigators suspect he's killed Ilan. As a result, they decide to suspend all negotiations until they receive a photo of Ilan, proving he's alive. The man promises to send it, and at the Anti-Crime Brigade they hope he'll walk into the trap they've set for him.

Yes, they hope he'll send the picture from one of the internet cafés where he created and checked his mailboxes, as they've set up surveillance cameras there. The police managed to trace these locations by obtaining from Hotmail the IP addresses associated with each email address. They sent them to Wanadoo, the internet service provider, who informed them that the person connected to the internet from three cybercafes, two in the Fourteenth Arrondissement, and one at Athis-Mons, near Paris.

A team from the Criminal Investigation Department of the Paris Police Prefecture also tried to collect fingerprints from the computers, as well as the wires the kidnapper used to connect his camera, but they didn't find anything worthwhile.

The IT fraud department checked the hard drives of the computers to see if there were traces of any other emails the criminal had sent. But HTML pages are volatile, and the investigators can't retrieve any data.

Their only chance of catching the man is to force him to return to one of these cybercafes, and by asking him to send another photo of Ilan, they hope to do just that.

Now, they're concealed and lying in wait, ready to ambush him. They know what kind of person they're looking for: The manager of one of the establishments saw the person who used the computer in question at the time the email was sent. According to him, he's an African-looking man, between twenty and thirty years old, about six feet tall. He was wearing a scarf that concealed the lower half of his face.

The only problem is the manager saw this man on Saturday,

and today is Tuesday. Yesterday, the investigators had located the kidnapper in Ivory Coast. Could the criminal possibly have taken a Paris-Abidjan flight on Sunday evening, for example, when we had no communication with him for several hours? All the police would have had to do was to check the passenger lists to know for sure . . .

It wouldn't have been an easy task, but it would have paid off. If they'd checked the passenger manifests, they'd have found him: Youssouf Fofana, age twenty-five, officially a resident of Bagneux, a repeat offender who had been arrested two weeks earlier for a violent crime and possession of a weapon. If they'd checked, he couldn't have escaped the notice of detectives at 36, quai des Orfèvres. But the investigators don't think of checking the flights for Abidjan or of informing the border police. Not for a second do they imagine that the kidnapper could be flying between the two countries.

They believe the gang consists of two totally distinct cells: one in France, the other in Ivory Coast. So the police lie in wait near the cybercafes mentioned above, convinced that the kidnapper will soon emerge. Well, they'll have a very long wait. The person the manager described has left Paris and put an accomplice in charge of taking and sending Ilan's photo. As an extra precaution, the accomplice sends the picture from a different cybercafe, in Arcueil, not directly to the common mailbox, but to the "brains" behind the gang, who's in Abidjan. In turn, the chief kidnapper creates a new email address from which to send the document.

It takes the investigators a while to work out the electronic trajectory this file followed (France, Ivory Coast, France) and meanwhile . . . like the file, the kidnapper has made a short return trip to Ivory Coast.

Day 5 ....

Behind the Scenes

Sworn to Silence

"THAT'S ENOUGH NOW, you have to stop talking about it and let us get on with it. I've got men hidden on boulevard Voltaire, all the salesmen are talking about nothing but Ilan, there are even text messages going around saying a young man's been kidnapped . . . If these shits are in the area and they hear anything, the situation may really deteriorate. We don't know what they're capable of, so tell your friends to shut up. If anyone asks you anything, everything's fine, Ilan's off on a trip somewhere, he's fine and you don't know anything else."

In the chief inspector's office, Deborah and Eve lower their gaze. They have been talking, it's true, but they thought it was the right thing to do. They thought the more of us there were looking for Ilan, the better our chances were of finding him. Well, no, these things don't work that way, so from now on, they've promised not to say a word. So have I. I won't say a thing to anyone, as the police themselves have asked me not to. They tell me to go back to work. To return to my normal life and to behave as if everything were fine.

Trusting and docile, I go back to my office. I say hello to my colleagues, I smile, I talk about everything and nothing, the sales that are almost over. I wear an expression for those who don't know, a tearless, carefree mask that crumbles in the night. All day I'm someone else. I play my role, and nothing shows through. I'm neither strong nor brave; I just do what's expected of me, as my son's life depends on it.

This masquerade is torture. I think constantly of the children who disappear on their way home from school, their parents who move heaven and earth . . . Why can't I do that, too? Why can't I speak to the press, post photos of my son all over the city, set up a hotline? Why are we prevented from doing any of the things people do in these situations? If only I'd been capable of disobeying . . .

Ilan's Ordeal

At Bagneux, Ilan is in hell. He's been tied up ever since his abduction; his jailors feed him with a straw. They allow him just enough to survive—high-protein diet drinks bought at the drugstore, a sandwich or biscuits when they remember and are willing to remove his gag. They haven't remembered for the last three days.

Sometimes they make him smoke dope to daze him, to keep him quiet. They hit him too . . . It's unbearable for me to have to write these words, to describe the terrible violence Ilan endured, but that's what they did to him. I can't ignore it. From now on I'll have to live with these images of my son being murdered, slowly, in an apartment in a Paris suburb, so close to my home. I have to continue to live and to hear his unending screams; I have to survive this onslaught . . .

They slap him, they bang his head, his back, his legs; they use the back of their hands or a broom handle. They soon use the same broom handle to stage a sodomy scene and to photograph him in a humiliating position. They go even further. On their leader's instructions, they slit his face with a blade, as the leader wants to send us a "gory" photo. Yes, they slit his handsome face, they disfigure him. The autopsy reveals a two-and-a-half-inch-long incision on his left cheek.

In addition to the beatings, the bullying, and the abuse, the conditions under which Ilan is held are a torture in themselves. The temperature outside is below freezing, the apartment isn't heated, and they've taken away all his clothes: his pullover, his T-shirt, his trainers, his socks, his jeans, his boxer shorts. To remove his leather jacket without removing the handcuffs, they cut through it with some schoolchildren's scissors. Ilan sleeps on the ground, on the orange sheet that was used as a backdrop in the first photo of him we received. His face is entirely covered in tape—"He looked like a mummy," one of the torturers admitted later—he can neither see nor speak; he can barely breathe.

We only realized just how cruel these monsters were when we discovered the second photograph of Ilan. It was sent to us yesterday to prove that he was still alive. Like the first, this snapshot shows him with a gun to his head, but this time he's completely naked. And the image is decorated with colorful balloons, like those on a "happy birthday" card. The persecutors are having fun. They're celebrating their victory. The victory of having captured a Jew, of being able to do what they want to him, and to murder him gleefully. Ilan, my treasure . . . their trophy.

✦

I don't know why they took off all his clothes. To humiliate him further? To force us to pay? To wash him, they were to say later. To get rid of any traces there might be on his body that could lead to them.

They were planning to release him earlier. They thought they would let him go after three days—that's why they took his clothes off so soon, but the negotiations got bogged down. They want their money by transfer, and the police refuse to give in to this demand. The psychologist working with Didier encourages him to hold out. She asks him to be stronger than them—this is what she said—"You have to be stronger than them. You have to maintain the upper hand." She orders him to break off the conversation when the kidnapper gets carried away. She congratulates him every time he refuses to give in. "Bravo, Didier, that's great. You're the one in control," she repeats, as Ilan grows weaker and weaker. Hungry, thirsty, pee, these are the only words he can now utter, and even this is too much: The neighbors may hear him.

Contrary to what I imagined, he's not being held in a house in a suburb of Abidjan, in an isolated bungalow in the middle of nowhere, or three floors underground, in a parking lot. He's in a two-bedroom apartment, on the third floor of one of the blocks of buildings on rue Serge Prokofiev, in Bagneux, in the Hauts-de-Seine neighborhood. An eleven-story block, inhabited by hundreds of people who take the elevator or the stairs every day and could, therefore, hear Ilan. But no one hears anything. No one notices anything. Not even all the young people popping in and out of a supposedly empty apartment.

The former tenants had vacated this two-bedroom apartment on January 16, and the new ones haven't moved in yet, but not one of the neighbors wonders what these people are doing there. None of the neighbors thinks they should inform the management company. Maybe because they know it would serve no purpose.

In July 2004, about twenty tenants had sent a petition to Domaxis, the company that owns the building, informing them that their residence had become the site of all kinds of deals: "We have heard that apartments that had been rented out are being squatted," they wrote, "and we notice a continual deterioration of our environment." The petition never received a reply, so much so that eighteen months later, the situation was exactly the same. "For months on end," one tenant told *Le Figaro,* "we notice that some of the common areas are occupied by strange people, visibly with the tacit agreement of the super."

In reality, the building super, thirty-nine years old, married, and the father of two children, did far more than give his "tacit approval": He placed the vacant apartment at the disposal of the criminals, even though members of the kidnapper's team had told him they were going to imprison someone there. Ilan was held in this first place for nine days, but at no time during that period did the super worry about what was happening to him. The only thing he was interested in was the 1,500 euros he'd been promised in exchange for this favor. And the only reason he finally asked the criminals to leave had nothing to do with any kind of humanitarian impulse: It was just because the painters were supposed to repaint the apartment before the future tenants arrived. Such a conscientious man! "I'm sorry, I apologize," this father of two children wrote to me once my son had been buried deep underground.

Omertà

Not a second goes by without my thinking of the lure. I seek her out in the faces of young girls I pass in the street, I talk to her constantly, in the bus or in my dreams. As I walk, yes, often as I walk I speak to her as if to God, I beg her to contact me. But my prayers are futile, because she was told to forget the whole thing. She's gone back to high school, and her classmate—the one who recruited her—makes sure she doesn't stumble. She reminds her regularly that what she did wasn't such a big deal.

Once the affair comes out in the press, this hustler even prepares a strategy to explain the group's actions in the event they were arrested: The lure just had to say she had been forced to do it because she was being threatened with rape; she found herself pregnant by a boy she met on the internet the very evening Ilan was kidnapped. This way, instead of being seen as an accomplice, she could play the victim. Reassured, the girl has kept her secret.

As for Lea, the girl who tried to seduce Maurice Keller, she also chooses to remain silent. During the first week of Ilan's ordeal, Lea's boyfriend, Jérôme Ribeiro, who is one of Ilan's captors, even told her another Jewish man had been kidnapped. He described, in the minutest detail, the dreadful conditions under which Ilan was being held, and, rather than informing the police, she chooses to share this awful secret with one of her friends. Monique Joly listens, makes no comment, then goes home. Now she knows a boy is being tortured just a few doors away from where she lives. Does it bother her in the least?

Jérôme Ribeiro also tells his other girlfriend, the "official" one. She contemplated going to the police, but Jérôme's parents forbid her to do so: They don't want their son to "pay for all the others."

And my son? Did Jérôme's parents spare a thought for my son? To protect their own son, they condemned mine to death.

How many people knew about the ordeal Ilan was suffering? How many knew he was being held captive on the third floor of 1 rue Serge Prokofiev at Bagneux, then in the cellar of a neighboring building? How many knew that he was being tortured, that he was being killed slowly? How many knew the people involved in this sinister enterprise? For my part, I discovered a number of them while leafing through *VSD* magazine a year after Ilan's death. Among them I saw Youssouf Fofana, Yahia Touré Kaba, Nabil Moustafa, Jérôme Ribeiro, Cédric Birot Saint-Yves, Guiri Oussivo N'Gazi, Francis Oussivo N'Gazi, Fabrice Polygone, Jean-Christophe Soumbou, Christophe Martin-Vallet, Jean-Christophe Gavarin, Samir Aït Abdelmalek, Sorour Arbabzadeh ("Emma"), Tiffen Gouret.

And that was nothing. Later, the investigators caught some other girls who had acted as lures, other accomplices, other people who knew and said nothing . . . Not forgetting all those who managed to slip through the police dragnet. How many are there? Those who heard a word, a sentence, a vague account of a kidnapping and imprisonment but who chose to continue on their way without a backward glance. For three weeks, dozens and dozens of people got on with their peaceful little lives while my son was being murdered. Barbarism always wears a human face.

Day 6

An Endless Struggle

Today Didier is instructed not to answer his phone. Negotiators from the Research and Intervention Brigade have decided to use this strategy to force the kidnapper to change his demands. The kidnapper has no intention of releasing Ilan until the ransom money has been transferred to his account. But, obviously, the investigators don't trust him. They're convinced that if we pay, the hostage will lose his "market value." He'll become a threat to the criminals he may be able to identify; therefore, for their own safety, it would be in their best interest to kill him.

So, between 8:30 and 9:30 this morning, Didier receives fourteen missed calls and two voice-mail messages on his cell phone. In the first message, the man tells him he's in a foul mood and he'd better hurry up. In the second message, he threatens to send a photo of Ilan covered in blood. Didier is finally allowed to answer his phone.

The negotiations start up again, but they still aren't going anywhere. The kidnapper won't budge, and for the umpteenth time he asks Didier to go to an unspecified location, accompanied by eleven people with their identity cards. Ilan's father refuses. He suggests a direct swap, the money for our son's release. The man goes crazy. He's insulting, violent, aggressive, and he threatens to harm Ilan. He even says he'll take him out to the forest in the trunk of a car, and in his email he writes:

> Soon you'll see a photo of Ilan with a broomstick up his ass. Bye

How does Didier withstand the shock? Keep calm and not collapse? He's falling apart inside, I know, just like me, who nonetheless continues to go to work every day. We've become robots. Puppets. Machines. We keep going despite ourselves. We're waiting for a miracle. Today, we really believed it had come . . .

In the middle of the afternoon, the kidnapper calls and, contrary to all expectations, announces that he doesn't want the money anymore. He tells us he is going to let Ilan go. He admits that he can no longer control "the others" and asks us to find some "middle ground."

Is he being sincere, or is this just a tactic to wreak havoc on our nerves? I think at that very moment, he really has had enough. Yes, I think he wants to be done with the whole thing, but he doesn't know how to end it. "We have to find some middle ground"—isn't that proof of his fatigue? He is clearly expressing his inability to resolve the situation, so why don't the police grab the hand he is holding out to us? Why don't they suggest something? Once again, they instruct Didier not to answer his cell, leaving the kidnapper to work himself up into a frenzy.

The result is that at 10:00 p.m. the man tells us, "They hurt

Ilan," and we'd soon receive the photo. In his final email he writes:

> Next time they're planning to do their worst. I can't control them any longer; cooperate or else. Reply quickly.

Day 7

Stratagems That Don't Work

Just Bluster

All night long the kidnapper harasses Didier. Between midnight and nine o'clock in the morning, he tries to call him about a dozen times, warning him again that if he doesn't answer, Ilan will be murdered and thrown into the woods. Didier doesn't take these threats lightly, but he obeys the police. They tell him not to answer . . . They say that if we don't answer, the criminal will be forced to agree to a "physical" meeting, rather than an online bank transfer. They're wrong. The man has no intention of changing his plans. He just changes interlocutors.

Now the kidnapper begins to badger Mony. He leaves a message on her voice mail, saying that if she wants her boyfriend dead, she's going about it in the right way. But Mony has also received instructions not to reply, so much so that, as a last resort, the kidnapper decides to call my apartment:

"I want to speak to Ruth Halimi."

"She isn't here, I'm her daughter," Eve replies.

"You're Ilan's sister?"

"Yes . . ."

"What's your dad up to? He doesn't get it or what? I'm gonna kill his son!"

"No, we've got the money, we have it," says Eve, to calm him down.

"It's the police who don't want to pay. I know."

"I'm going to call my father; we'll find a solution . . ."

"You know what we did to Ilan yesterday? He was subjected to depraved acts, so what are you waiting for? We did perverted things to him."

In a panic, Eve immediately contacts the Quai des Orfèvres to tell them about the call. The chief inspector tells her to stay put and not to pick up the phone again before the negotiators arrive. My daughter obeys. The phone doesn't stop ringing, but she doesn't answer. And it's torture for her. The man who's holding her brother captive is on the other end of the line. He seems to be about her age. Maybe she'd be able to find the right words . . . She's not allowed to. Alone in the apartment she presses her hands to her ears to block out the cursed ringing, to resist the desire to answer, and to do as the police say. She feels bad about it for a long time afterward.

Didier turns up at my apartment with negotiators and psychologists. Within a few minutes the living room is transformed into a wiretap operations center. They instruct Ilan's father to be harsh and uncompromising. Once again, he has to have "the upper hand" and not let them see he's afraid. So he talks to the kidnapper as if he were lecturing a child. He asks him to calm down, and when the man insults him, he hangs up.

The psychologist congratulates him. She tells him he's done well. "You're perfect."

Eve and I watch the scene from the corridor, and we're stunned. "You're stronger than he is." "You're the one in control." "You have the upper hand," repeats the psychologist. Who does she think she can convince of that? They have our son. He's more precious to us than anything else, and we have nothing. Nothing but bluster. Who bluffs when a human life is at stake?

The Investigators' Big Mistake

What are the police up to? They don't want to inform the media, they refuse to put out identikit photos of the two lures—Lea and the "brunette"—and they ask us to say nothing to anyone and force Didier to be uncompromising. It's exactly a week since Ilan was abducted, and the kidnapper's going crazy, so why don't the police change their strategy?

Because they don't, for an instant, imagine that the kidnapper will kill my son. That's the investigators' big mistake. They've completely misread this man's profile. They think they are dealing with one of the stalwarts of organized crime, someone experienced and who has certain ethics, when in fact they're dealing with a vulgar housing-project delinquent who fears neither God nor man. They believe this crime is financially motivated, when it is above all anti-Semitic. They don't realize that the anti-Semitic aspect of this whole affair is far more than a minor detail. Recognizing this might have encouraged them to treat the kidnapper differently, to define his psychological profile properly, and to evaluate the risks Ilan was facing. If they had understood these men's hatred, they would have realized that Ilan could die. But the investigators don't grasp this hatred—or even their own limitations. Despite successive failures, they remain convinced they will catch the kidnapper. They think they are cleverer than he is. And all this while their investigation has barely progressed.

The attempts to identify the phones don't lead anywhere, as the kidnapper makes sure he calls from pay phones. Now, because of the free market, his calls are automatically transmitted via the cheapest operators used by the pay-phone company. In other words, Fofana's calls are routed through numerous gateways based in England, Italy, or the Netherlands before reaching us. To identify the source of the call, the police have to make as many international requests as there are gateway links, which makes it nearly impossible for them to be able to pinpoint where the criminal is at a particular time.

As for the cybercafes where he connected to the internet, it takes the police a long time to locate them. To start with, they identify the IP address connected to the message, that is to say the numeric code showing the references of the computer used, as well as the data indicating the time and date stamp of the connection. Then they send this IP address to the access provider, asking them to provide the criminal's geographic location.

Although the Wanadoo employees have been informed of the situation, they demand that the police fax them a court order before providing the slightest information. They justify their response by the company's moral obligation not to violate its customers' privacy. This is a huge waste of time for the investigators. And time is so precious.

Once they have begun to monitor the cybercafes, the investigators have to deal with the kidnapper's tricks: He connects from a different place every time he calls. But despite these technical difficulties, the detectives at the Quai des Orfèvres don't give up.

They are very hopeful that the ongoing investigation will come to a successful conclusion.

Red Herrings: The Hustler and the Rap World

Investigations into Jules Huet's telephone line (his phone had been stolen), the one Lea had used to seduce Maurice Keller, leads to another victim, Jean Loiselle, who has also been contacted by the lure. This boy reveals that on January 14 a girl contacted him, seeking an amorous meeting. She claimed her name was Natacha and she'd met him briefly near the Hotel Georges V. She said she was a stripper. Loiselle, who's in a stable relationship, refused her advances. But intrigued by the phone call, he called her back to find out how she obtained his number. She didn't answer.

During his interview, Loiselle says he thinks he may have met this girl at the end of December at Hustler, a strip club in the Eighth Arrondissement. Now the investigators have discovered that Keller and Ilan have both been to this trendy club on separate occasions. This leads them to assume that the kidnappers worked the Hustler to choose their next hostage.

The police bureau in charge of sex trafficking sets to work right away. They question the staff at this establishment, discreetly set up an undercover operation, and create a file of 150 photos of women to show Loiselle and Keller, hoping they can identify the lure.

In another operation, the Anti-Crime Brigade decides to question all the rap groups in the area of Val-de-Marne, because they've just received an anonymous letter implicating rappers in Ilan's kidnapping. It turns out that the kidnapper is eventually filmed at one of the monitored internet cafés wearing an Adedi sweatshirt, a brand popular in the rap world. This gives the investigators every reason to believe the anonymous information might be credible, especially since one of the singers mentioned has a criminal background. A judge in Créteil has already issued an arrest warrant for him to be questioned in connection with a homicide investigation.

Although the Hustler and rap world trails don't lead anywhere, they occupy all the detectives at the Quai des Orfèvres, who are convinced they are valid. And this activity gives them good reason to refuse the kidnapper's offers, as they hope to delay any further negotiations. Meanwhile, my son is still being tortured.

March 20, 2018

LYONS, Ill.—Arthur Jones, longtime Holocaust denier and former head of the American Nazi Party, wins the Republican nomination for Illinois's Third Congressional District. Jones has also been associated with the conspiratorial and anti-Semitic Populist Party and the National Socialist White People's Party. The candidate's campaign language paired "America First" rhetoric with outright Holocaust denial, and his website included a section titled "The Holocaust Racket," which argued that "Organized World Jewry" perpetrated "the biggest, blackest lie in history."

Day 8

Our First Shabbat without Ilan

I HEAR HIS voice, his footsteps in the corridor, and I think, That's it. Ilan's home.

"Is he back?" I ask the two officers dozing on the sofa.

I must have seemed crazy, dressed in my nightdress, my hair all over the place. I must have been a pitiful sight standing in the doorway at 4:00 a.m.; there was such hopelessness in their expressions …

Every night I wake with a start. I hear him, I see him, I feel him. I have the same recurring dream: I see heavy stone doors, like the doors of a vault, opening and closing. So I run into the living room, and, like a soothsayer, I question the police officers: "Do you know a town where there's a cemetery? Ilan is near it, I'm sure, I saw it in a dream …"

I'm going mad. Knowing my son is being tortured and not being able to do anything about it is physically unbearable. And this eternal waiting, with its hopes and its disappointments, its meetings that are constantly delayed, missed, canceled, are eating away at me slowly. I glean snippets of the investigation in the meandering conversations I have with the policemen. I hear everything about rap, nightclubs, other lures, other victims, but I understand nothing.

✦

In despair, Eve decides to go and see a rabbi, taking a photo of Ilan with her, so that he can pray for him. The rabbi tells her that the previous month the son of another Jewish family had been kidnapped. The family was asked to pay a ransom of 100,000 euros. Fearing for her son's life, the mother had refused to call the police, despite the rabbi's advice. But she had called him back a few days later to thank him and to tell him that her son had been released. The rabbi doesn't know whether they paid. Nor can he tell us the lady's name; she didn't tell him. He will pray for Ilan.

I immediately inform the police that another Jew had been kidnapped, and the police promise to investigate. They question the rabbi but don't find the victim or his mother. They abandon this lead. I feel so alone, so helpless . . . The only thing that keeps me going is prayer, and, on this first Shabbat without Ilan, I pray fervently. Yes, I pray. I beg for news, just some news, as we no longer have any. Since yesterday afternoon, the kidnapper hasn't sent us anything—neither emails nor phone calls—and I'm terrified at the idea that he has carried out his threats. The last time we heard from him he told us he was going to kill Ilan, dump him in the trunk of a car, and throw his body in the woods. The two policemen who are spending the evening with me assure me that he won't do any such thing.

Are they really convinced of this, or are they merely trying to reassure me? They're kind, these two policemen, friendly and compassionate. But what can they do? They're as helpless, furious, and enraged as we are. As the days go by, some of the officers have almost become a part of the family. We have dinner together, they accompany me to the supermarket, come running with me when I can't bear sitting around in my apartment any longer. I spend long hours talking to them about Ilan. I tell them how happy I was to have had a son after two girls. I remember his first years when I took him to Brittany with his sisters, for the holidays . . . The memories flood back. My little boy in a yellow slicker against the blue of the ocean, his face full of sleep when he used to slip into my bed early in the morning, his piping voice reading the *parashah* on the day of his bar mitzvah, and then, later, this handsome young man in a suit who offered me his arm at my daughter's wedding. I was so proud of him . . .

It hasn't always been easy to make ends meet. I raised my three children on my own, but they never wanted for anything, least of all love. Maybe that's why Ilan was not a distrustful person . . . He was a boy who liked people—and I'm not saying that because he's dead and I'm idealizing him. I used to think that about him when he was alive, too. Yes, Ilan truly liked other people. He was curious about them, he was concerned about them, he reached out to them. He had all kinds of friends. Whether they were Jewish, Muslim, Catholic, or Buddhist wasn't important to Ilan: He saw them first and foremost as fellow humans. Brothers. He trusted in human beings, and it's this trust that killed him.

I'm angry at him for having been so careless.

I spend my time telling him over and over again, in my head and out loud, How could you have been so reckless? Everyone close to me refuses to listen to me saying things like that. They swear that Ilan had no reason not to follow this girl: Any boy of his age would have agreed to go to her place for a drink . . . I'm sure they're right, but I continue to blame my son. I need to talk to him all the time, as if he were here in front of me; otherwise his voice will take over and I'll hear him scream my name. Yes, I hear him shouting Mom, as I know very well that, when they're suffering, men call out for their mothers. And I, his mother, can do nothing for him.

September 2012

STAMFORD, Conn.—Melanie Roloff walked into her fourth-grade classroom and noticed two classmates looking at her and laughing. That was the start of months of harassment. "I was called a poor and dirty Jew if I brought matzah to school on Passover, or dreidels to share with my friends on Chanukah," Roloff wrote in an essay. "I was told I belonged in the Holocaust, in the ovens." When Roloff told her tormentors to back off, she was sent to the office for disrupting the class. She reached out to the Anti-Defamation League for help, and later became a trainer and spokesperson for the organization's "Words to Action" program (then known as "Confronting Anti-Semitism").

Day 9

Messages to the Rabbi

Although we've had no news at all since Friday evening, Rabbi Théo Zarquette is about to hear from the kidnappers. We don't know this man, we don't go to his synagogue, but he's Jewish, and the kidnapper wants to speak to a Jew.

On this Sunday, Rabbi Zarquette spends a cheerful evening in the company of his family at a bar mitzvah in Seine Saint-Denis. Toward midnight he decides to go home and collects his overcoat from the cloakroom. As he slips his hands into his pockets, he realizes that he had left his mobile phone in one of them. He glances at it and sees that someone has left him three messages.

At 10:05 p.m. this call had come in:

"Hello, good evening. A Jew has been kidnapped. You're a rabbi. Answer this email. We want an answer as soon as possible. As proof, you'll find a cassette in the apartment house next to your synagogue, in Aimée Nicolas's mailbox."

At 10:20 p.m.:

"Hello! You're a rabbi. A Jewish believer has been . . ."

At 10:20 p.m.:

"Hello! Go quickly to this address. In Aimée Nicolas's mailbox there's a cassette recorded by a Jew who's been kidnapped. Look quickly at internet, too. We won't tolerate any kind of slipup—none!"

Hoping it's just a hoax, Rabbi Zarquette takes the calls seriously. He tells his brother-in-law, a lawyer, about them, and the rabbi's brother-in-law advises him to go to a police station immediately.

The police accompany him to the Quai des Orfèvres, and his statement is taken in the early hours of Monday, January 30. He's never heard the name Ilan Halimi before and doesn't recognize his photograph, either. He doesn't understand why the kidnappers have contacted him. But the messages on his cell phone are nonetheless clear: It's a Jew who's been kidnapped. And he, the rabbi, is the "ultimate Jew." He's the "bearded guy with a *kippah*," as Youssouf Fofana puts it later during one of his criminal hearings, the representative of a community that the anti-Semitic cliché defines as rich and close-knit. To an anti-Semite, the rabbi seems to be in the best position to collect the funds required for a Jew's release.

The investigators attempt to connect to the electronic address specified in the message, but as the password is wrong, or the sender has made a mistake somewhere, they are unable to. Assisted by crime scene technicians, the Anti-Crime Brigade goes to Nicolas's address. In her mailbox she does, in fact, find a package addressed to the rabbi: The envelope contains an audiocassette.

On this tape, his voice weak and hesitant, Ilan states his identity. He says: "I am Ilan, Ilan Halimi. I'm the son of Halimi Didier and Halimi Ruth. I'm a Jew and I'm being held hostage."

Yet again, how could they not make the connection with journalists who are being held prisoner by religious fanatics? How do they not think of Daniel Pearl, forced, like Ilan, to face the camera and repeat that he was Jewish? Does it even cross the detectives' minds? Do they finally realize that I've been right all along? Do they acknowledge the kidnapper's anti-Semitic motives? No. They draw no conclusions from this tape. And I'm the only one haunted by the tragic end of the great Jewish reporter, Pearl, beheaded in Karachi, Pakistan, in 2002, while on assignment for the *Wall Street Journal.*

Ilan pauses after each word. Beside him, someone strikes a piece of furniture, probably a table, on which the text he is reading has been placed ... No, I'm wrong. On both the photos we received he was blindfolded; he cannot see. So it's him they're beating. In fact, he moans. Not just because he's scared, but also because he's being tortured.

"I'm being held hostage," he murmurs, "nine days and I'm asking the rabbi to help, please sir ... They're going to kill me, don't leave me here ... please ... please, I need help ... I can't bear it any longer. Mom, please ... don't leave me here alone ... don't leave me, please. Give them anything they want, give them money ... anything they want, please. I can't hold out any longer dear God."

Hearing my son pleading like this, feeling the exhaustion and distress in his voice, the ordeal he's suffering, realizing he's terrified at the idea that we may abandon him, is far greater torment than any of the photos we see. How can we prove that we're there for him? How can we let him know he's not alone ...?

The cassette is placed under seal and handed over to the engineers at the Scientific Police Laboratory in Paris to search for fingerprints or other biological evidence, but they find nothing. As for the recording, it's sent to the laboratory for signal analysis and treatment, in hopes that some of the audio elements will reveal something new. Another false hope.

Detectives at the Anti-Crime Brigade question Nicolas. They ask her to explain how the cassette happened to be delivered to her mailbox. This ordinary young girl, who lives in a chic neighborhood of the capital, is stunned. She doesn't know anyone called Ilan Halimi, she has no friends who work in cell-phone shops, she doesn't go to strip clubs, has received no anonymous phone calls, and noticed no suspicious characters in the hallway of her building. She doesn't understand why she's been chosen as the recipient of such a package. In all probability there's nothing to understand, beyond the fact that she lives a few steps away from the phone booth the criminal used to contact the rabbi . . . Before leaving the three messages, he must have pushed open the first door to an apartment building entrance that was unlocked and slipped his envelope at random into a mailbox.

A Paris Police Crime Brigade team also checks the phone booth for fingerprints, but they don't find anything there, either: The man always takes care not to leave any evidence behind. As for finding any witnesses among the neighbors, there aren't any. It's a residential neighborhood that's completely deserted on Sunday evenings.

The police nonetheless identify a hotel near the phone booth that has a surveillance camera. They ask to see the tapes, but the camera is positioned next to a streetlight, so after dark the tape only captures a blinding white light. One can just about make out a few silhouettes . . . Once again, the kidnapper lucks out.

Day 10

The Move to the Cellar

At 4:00 a.m. today, Ilan leaves the apartment where he has been held for nine days. Or, rather, he is moved to the boiler room of a neighboring building, located at 4, rue Serge Prokofiev in Bagneux.

The kidnapper came all the way back from Abidjan to manage the move himself. He has no choice, as the new tenants of the two-bedroom apartment are soon to move in. The investigation later reveals that, for a while, he has thought of moving Ilan to the home of one of his girlfriends who had "kindly" made her residence available to him. But they would have had to cross Paris with the hostage in the trunk of a car; it was too great a risk.

So the kidnapper chooses to take him somewhere close by, to the basement of 4, rue Serge Prokofiev. He leaves the apartment with my son, trussed and gagged, hoisted onto his back. He passes the adjacent apartments, takes the elevator, and crosses the hallway of the building. Once again, no one hears anything. It is late at night, I am later told. Ilan couldn't shout, and his jailors, positioned at strategic points, are on the lookout. Can I believe that no one saw anything or heard anything? Yes, I have to believe it; otherwise I'd never believe anything ever again . . .

Outside, the street is deserted and silent. The kidnapper moves on to the main road. He travels a few hundred yards with his hostage over his shoulder like an ordinary bag of dirty laundry. Does a neighbor catch a glimpse of them? A passerby? Someone driving a car? They're in the street, in plain view, but once again no one notices them. And once again, for the same reasons, I have to believe this . . .

Ilan is imprisoned in a basement. Now there's almost no chance that anyone will hear him, and the conditions under which he is held continue to deteriorate. Still tied up, and wearing only a white dressing gown, he is subjected to temperatures far colder than in the unheated apartment. As there are no toilets here, he has to ask for a bottle or a plastic bag every time he wants to relieve himself. Some jailors refuse to give one to him, hoping whoever takes over from them will deal with this thankless job. And when Ilan can't wait any longer, his torturers make things worse for him. They'd only been hired for three days, and now they can't stand having to guard him any longer. So they take their rage out on my son, as if he were responsible for his extended captivity.

Ilan becomes the target of their vitriol.

✦

A second week without Ilan begins, and, following the instructions I received from the police, I continue to go to work. I sit at my receptionist's desk, and I answer the phone. I know some of the callers, so I try to sound normal. I pretend.

The switchboard handles no less than one hundred lines

that ring incessantly. But my direct line has not rung yet. It's only ever used by people who know me, people who work here, a few friends, my daughters, and, of course, Ilan. It's on this number that the kidnappers decide to call me at 10:30 a.m.

"You're Ilan's mom?" asks a boy.

"Yes . . ."

"If you want to see him alive again, call [the rabbi's number] immediately. If you want to see him alive again," he repeats, "call this number immediately; otherwise, we'll kill him on Wednesday."

The call only lasts a few seconds, but I'm trembling from head to foot. It's the first time I've spoken directly to the kidnappers. And I didn't have time to reply. There are no words to describe the state I'm in. Terror is nothing compared to what I'm feeling. He said, "We'll kill him on Wednesday," and I know he's not lying. I know he's capable of it; his voice on the phone was so determined.

In my panic, I call the chief inspector, who's asked us to inform him immediately if we're contacted. He instructs me not to answer the phone again and to stay where I am.

A few moments later, two of his officers come to get me. They take me to the Quai des Orfèvres, where I am to write down the precise content of my conversation with the kidnapper.

The email address and the code I was given provide access to the email originally intended for the rabbi. This is what the kidnapper wrote:

> It's 9 days ago a Jew was kidnapped and the ransom hasn't been payed we want 350,000 euros for his release, and if this sum isn't ready by the 1.02.06 we'll execute ilan you can call his parents or his father. I'm expecting you to say yes by replying to this email address before 10 tomorrow morning

> if theres isn't an answer, it will be consider as programming Ilans death. go check what I send you and what I tell you.

✦

So my son is reduced to nothing—neither a boy, nor a cell-phone salesman, not even a Frenchman. Nothing but a Jew. And for this reason I know he won't make it. I know the kidnappers will beat Ilan to death since, the way they see it, a Jew isn't a member of the human community. He deserves no pity. So I beg the detectives to pay, even if we have no guarantee that they'll release Ilan when they get the money. I'm ready to take this risk. I can no longer bear knowing they have Ilan. But the police won't listen to me; they completely ignore the extent of this anti-Semitic hatred. As long as they aren't almost 100 percent certain the kidnapper will bring Ilan with him, they refuse all the meetings he suggests.

✦

The electronic message intended for the rabbi was sent from an internet café on boulevard Brune in the Fourteenth Arrondissement. And the calls Didier and I received this morning were made from phone booths also located in this area. So the kidnapper is wandering around freely in this part of Paris, and the police can't catch him.

Finally, the Anti-Crime Brigade decides to set up a mobile surveillance and capture unit near the above mentioned places. But the kidnapper continues to mock us . . . Early in the afternoon he calls me again at my office. This time the police allow me to answer it. This time the kidnapper finally lets me speak to my son.

"Hello, Mom . . ." says Ilan.

That's the last time I hear his voice.

Day 11

Contacting the Jewish Cousin

Although the rabbi doesn't respond to his demands, the kidnapper continues to believe the Jewish community is rich and stands together. This anti-Semitic prejudice is so deeply embedded that he's convinced that one member of the community will pay to save the life of another. So he decides to contact another Jew, someone close to us this time. He chooses Daniel, Ilan's cousin.

In the late afternoon, my nephew is wandering through the aisles of a department store with one of his friends when his cell phone rings.

"You don't know me," a man says to him, "you don't know who we are. I know you're Daniel. Go to the dry cleaner around the corner from your house. There's an envelope there for you."

Daniel, who has no idea what's going on since we've all been sworn to secrecy, asks his caller whether this is some kind of joke, but the latter hangs up before Daniel can finish his sentence.

Probably largely out of curiosity Daniel and his friend go to the address they've been given. Daniel chooses to wait in front of the dry cleaner, and it's his friend who goes inside.

"Has someone given you something for Daniel?" he asks the man behind the counter.

"Yes," replies the dry cleaner, handing over an envelope.

Daniel, who's watching through the window, goes into the shop.

"Did they leave it a long time ago?"

"Just about an hour."

"Do you remember the person who gave it to you?"

"It was a young man . . . black guy."

"What did he say to you?"

"Nothing special. I asked if you were a client. He said no, but you'd come by to collect the envelope."

As soon as he's out in the street again, Daniel opens the package. It contains an audiocassette and a Polaroid photograph, cut out in the shape of a triangle. The snapshot shows a naked person lying on a bed. He's holding a copy of a newspaper, *L'Équipe*, in his handcuffed hands. As his face is completely hidden under a layer of tape, Ilan's cousin is unable to identify him.

Since he has no idea what all this is about, Daniel decides to go home to listen to the audio recording. The sound quality of the tape is very bad, but he nonetheless manages to hear: "It's Ilan."

Unnerved, my nephew doesn't listen to the rest. He puts the photo and the cassette back into the envelope and rushes to his stepfather's. Together they listen to the whole recording.

Just as he did on the audiocassette sent to the rabbi, but this time in an even weaker voice, Ilan asks, begs, calls for help. And he instructs Daniel to connect to a particular email address.

"You have to go to the BAC, the Anti-Crime Brigade, immediately," his stepfather tells him.

Daniel follows his advice and also tries to contact me. He gets through in the early evening, after he's made his statement and a police officer is taking him to the Quai des Orfèvres.

"Some guy called me," he says. "He asked me to go to a dry cleaner, which I did. There was an envelope addressed to me there, and inside a photo of Ilan with a cassette, on which he begs me to pay. What's going on?"

"I can't talk at the moment; I'll call back later to explain."

"He's being held hostage?"

"Yes . . . It's been ten days. I'll call you back, Daniel, I can't speak now."

"But why?"

"I'll call you back."

✦

The Anti-Crime Brigade has instructed me to say nothing at all to anyone. And, like an obedient soldier, I don't even dare answer my nephew. I'm scared to go against police instructions. Throughout this terrible ordeal, I'm like a little girl—I believe everything I'm told, and I've been told that if I were to talk I may never see my son again. So I keep quiet. I grit my teeth and smother my desire to tell the press. I trust the investigators.

At the Quai des Orfèvres, Daniel is interviewed by a detective who spends two hours taking his statement. Daniel knows nothing that can help the investigation.

As for the email he's been told to read, it's like all the emails we've received so far: The kidnapper demands his ransom, but doesn't say how it's to be paid. He only says that the "day it is to be handed over" should be this Thursday. A day later than the deadline set in the message addressed to the rabbi.

✦

The investigators discover that this email was sent at about midday from an internet café on rue d'Alésia—the Fourteenth Arrondissement again! Why isn't this establishment being monitored? Why doesn't the chief inspector in charge of the case have men lying in wait around the shop? For the last eleven days, the criminal has been using all the internet cafés in the area, never the same one twice, so there was a very high chance that he'd go to the one on rue d'Alésia! The man is scared of nothing and no one; he's still strolling around Paris! He even had the nerve to drop the letter off at the dry cleaner himself...

March 29, 2016

PRINCETON, N.J.—Neo-Nazi Andrew Auernheimer hacks into printers at universities around the country, sending out a raft of hateful, anti-Semitic propaganda. Auernheimer is associated with the white supremacist website the *Daily Stormer* and has a history of similar cyberattacks. Universities nationwide condemn the attacks and pledge to address holes in their security protocols, while also working to ensure the safety of their students. Maya Wahrman, a senior at Princeton University, one of the targeted schools, told the *Washington Post*, "It's . . . scary . . . that someone would care so much about hating Jews to hack an elaborate printer system across the country."

Day 12

The Dry Cleaner's Confirmation

When he's questioned, the dry cleaner gives a very precise description of the suspected kidnapper. It coincides with the statement made by one of the internet café managers: The man is of African or West Indian descent, very dark-skinned, about twenty-three or twenty-four years old, about five foot seven, and quite slim.

The Anti-Crime Brigade has had his description for the last week, the dry cleaner only confirmed it, but they still haven't thought it worthwhile to send it out to the other police stations. So it's quite by chance that the team of police officers patrolling avenue de Ternes yesterday at about 5:00 p.m. stopped the man called Youssouf Fofana. Finding his behavior suspicious—and with good reason, he's just dropped off his envelope!—the officers ask him for his ID papers. But everything's in order. And because they haven't been informed of the case that's occupying the whole of the Quai des Orfèvres, they let this ideal suspect go! I can imagine how hard Ilan's kidnapper laughed at the police that day . . . and how strong and invincible he must have felt. So invincible that, for another thirteen days, he continues to beat my son.

Day 13

A Trap Fails

As at the outset, the police decide that Didier will be the kidnapper's only contact, so they tell Daniel not to answer his cell phone. They hope to force the man to call Ilan's father again. Apart from two laconic calls this past Monday, Didier hasn't heard from the kidnapper for six days now.

This morning, the Anti-Crime Brigade gets lucky: The kidnapper contacts Didier. There's a feverish exchange of emails, and, given the difficulties encountered with the service providers, the investigators throw themselves into a race against time to pinpoint the internet cafés used. As usual, the kidnapper changes location after every call. The Quai des Orfèvres increases its surveillance operation and sends all its staff out into the field. The policemen, the officers, the lieutenants of all the brigades are sent out to watch what they consider the nerve points.

At 12:30 p.m. the kidnapper sends yet another email to Didier: This time he threatens to mutilate our son. He sends this message from the internet café he used earlier to send us a photo of Ilan. It's the first time he's using the same place twice. The manager of this business, who described him to the investigators, recognizes him. The manager immediately informs the Anti-Crime Brigade of the suspect's presence.

Utter chaos ensues. All the Quai des Orfèvres' staff are out lying in wait, but none of them are close enough to this internet café to arrest the suspect. A uniformed team patrolling the sector is asked to intervene. They're told to go immediately to 9, rue Poirier-de-Narçay in the Fourteenth Arrondissement, to arrest a man of African descent, aged about twenty-three or twenty-four, about five foot seven. The urgency of the situation doesn't leave these patrolmen any time to find out more. They don't know the person in question is involved in a kidnapping and imprisonment case. They have no idea how dangerous he is, nor are they aware of the difficulties the Anti-Crime Brigade has faced over the last thirteen days. So a large team, with their caps and their truncheons, launches into the street they were sent to, taking no precautions and making no effort to conceal their presence. They hurry along, eyes glued to the facades, as they search for the number they were given. Like most businesses, the internet café is not numbered, so they rush past it into the hallway of the adjoining building.

Through the shop window Ilan's kidnapper watches all these policemen hurry by, and he realizes that they're there for him. So, as discreetly as possible, he slips away. Obviously, they don't find anyone at number 9, so the police leave the building. And then, at the end of the road, they see the silhouette of a man who fits the description they've been given. They realize he must be the suspect, since he's now running away. They give chase, but the criminal is already out of reach, and he races off at top speed. The police are unable to catch up with him.

How could the Anti-Crime Brigade, with its reputation for professionalism and efficiency, have let him get away? Their men were already staking out other internet cafés. I'm told, they couldn't be everywhere. Maybe, but why haven't the Parisian police stations been informed of Ilan's kidnapping?

If they had been, the policemen on patrol would certainly have been a bit more discreet. If they'd known about the emails we'd already received, they wouldn't have wasted their time rushing into the hallway of a building! Why would they? They would have blocked off the street to start with. They could have stormed the internet café and picked the criminal up, as easily as picking a flower! Even in bad TV shows the police know how to do that... Why was the Anti-Crime Brigade silent? Why did they work alone? Did they think they were so good they didn't need anyone's help? Although they tried to make up for this glaring mistake the next morning by sending a wanted notice for Fofana to all the police stations, they were not to have another opportunity to apprehend him. He never connected to the internet from a cybercafe in the Paris region again.

Day 14

The Wanted Poster

THEY LOST HIM. He was there, within reach, and they couldn't manage to arrest him! How can we trust them now? How can we keep our hopes up? Personally, I no longer have any hope. And yet, all is not lost. Thanks to the surveillance camera, discreetly placed inside the internet café on rue Poirier-de-Narçay, we now know what the kidnapper looks like. The investigators have extracted a photograph from the film. The kidnapper fits the descriptions provided by the dry cleaner and the manager of the internet café: black, quite young looking, about five foot seven, of fairly slight build. He's wearing a hooded sweatshirt that covers his head. It's a black Adedi sweatshirt, a brand the urban music world appreciates. The logo that looks like a tag is written in large white capital letters across the chest: UNFORGETTABLE.

After yesterday's fiasco the detectives finally decide to send this photo out to all the police stations and all the operational headquarters. So, this morning, the chiefs of all the departmental headquarters for public security in the inner periphery receive a "wanted" notice. In turn, they are supposed to pass it on to all their scattered services. Staff from the Anti-Crime Brigade go personally to each of the operational units in the Paris region to ensure that the information is properly passed on to everyone in the field. Meetings are held in every police station, and all the heads of every department are present: the general service, the community policing service, the investigative unit, the Anti-Crime Brigade.

Since Ilan's mobile phone last pinged off a cell tower in Sceaux, the investigators ask the police stations in the Hauts-de-Seine to be particularly watchful. In Bagneux they show the suspect's picture to local police officers, asking them to look at it closely, but they're sure they've never seen him.

However, three weeks earlier, on January 11 to be precise, this man had spent the night in their jail. He had been arrested for carrying a knife and had been photographed by the police services for their records. So these policemen have a photo of the kidnapper in their desk drawers. And the picture is a recent one—I repeat, they had taken it just three weeks before! Did they consult their files? Did they compare the picture they were shown with the photographs of the delinquents on record? What for? "I'm telling you, we've never set eyes on the guy," they say. And once again the criminal slips through the net . . . Nonetheless, the police have known him since he turned sixteen, as he's already been involved in thirteen cases.

Day 15

Waiting

Day 16

Waiting

Day 17

Back and Forth

Mounting Anxiety

After his close shave with the police last week, the kidnapper decides to back off. We hear nothing from him until today, and our anxiety has been mounting. This is the second weekend that goes by with no news, leaving us to imagine the worst: They've decided to carry out the threats made throughout the previous week, to the rabbi, to my nephew Daniel, to Didier, to me . . . In our heads, the hostage-taker's words play back in a loop—Ilan covered in blood, Ilan mutilated, Ilan brutally murdered, Ilan driven off in the trunk of a car and dumped in the woods.

The police aren't feeling very optimistic either. Fully aware of their failure, they fear that Thursday's failed trap may have pushed the criminal to kill his hostage. The officers staying with me don't know what to say. They hardly dare meet my eyes.

A Glimmer of Hope

But this morning, the kidnapper finally makes contact with Didier again. What a relief to hear his voice and to realize there's still hope . . . If he demands money, it means Ilan must still be alive.

The man suggests a meeting that very day, at place de Clichy. This time he doesn't demand that Didier come with a laptop computer connected to Wi-Fi, accompanied by eleven people with their identity cards. So this means he agrees to the idea of releasing Ilan in exchange for the ransom. It's the first time. The detectives think it's a serious offer: Didier promises to be there.

At the stipulated time, Ilan's father goes to place de Clichy. Me, I'm at my office and I'm bubbling over with impatience. The nightmare's finally drawing to an end; it's a question of hours now. Life will go back to being what it was before, and we'll move on, Ilan will forget this hell; he'll forget all about it, I promise myself.

Didier has assured the kidnapper he'll bring the money, but this is a purely rhetorical promise: The French police follow a policy of never giving in to blackmail, so they have given Didier no money. The only purpose of this meeting is to trap the criminal. The Quai des Orfèvres has set up an operation on an unprecedented scale. Dozens of policemen are posted all over the place, in the square, in cafés, businesses, on the main roads leading to the square, and they're all discreetly concealed. The whole area is locked down.

But no one turns up at the given time. Didier waits; the minutes go by, still nothing. The policemen hold their breath.

The kidnapper finally calls. But it's to delay the meeting. The investigators have the feeling he won't come. They nonetheless agree to this second offer, but, as they fear, the kidnapper doesn't show up.

The Kidnapper's Second Trip to Ivory Coast

The reason the criminal didn't turn up at place de Clichy is because he'd already left for Ivory Coast two days ago. Very soon the investigators pinpoint the origin of his calls and his emails: They're coming from publiphones and internet cafés in Abidjan. And in fact, since Thursday, there's been no communication from the kidnapper originating from France.

The theory that he's left French territory for the second time seems plausible, but the investigators don't put much stock in it, any more than they did two weeks ago. How is it that these seasoned professionals, familiar with criminal behavior, don't, for a moment, imagine this scenario? How could they have been so blind on both occasions? The man who contacted us from Abidjan could only have been the same as the one calling us from Paris. We never received calls from Africa and France on the same day. And then, whether he was in Paris or Abidjan, the man had exactly the same voice, used the same expressions . . . He must have been traveling between the two countries. But no, the Quai des Orfèvres continues to believe we're dealing with a network that consists of two totally separate units, and no one checks the lists of passengers on flights to Abidjan this time either. However, on one of the passenger lists, there's a certain Youssouf Fofana, twenty-five years old, a resident of Bagneux, and known to the police force for thirteen legal proceedings. Can anyone really believe that this profile wouldn't have alerted the investigators?

Late in the afternoon, after the two missed meetings at place de Clichy, the kidnapper instructs Didier to go to Brussels. There, he's to meet a man who'll confirm the ransom amount. So the criminal has an accomplice in Belgium . . .

Didier is given no guarantees regarding Ilan's release, and he refuses to go. The kidnapper then makes another totally outlandish request: He asks Didier to make a transfer via Western Union.

Yet again, the man sees the payment of the ransom as a precondition for the hostage's release. He repeats it over and over again: First we send the money, and then he'll give us back our son. He's no longer open to the idea of a simultaneous swap. The investigators find this demand excessive and unacceptable. They maintain their initial position; they think that if we pay, the kidnapper will no longer have any reason to keep Ilan alive.

This day, which had begun with such hope, ends in a stalemate, with the man voicing even more ferocious threats and insults:

> Just wait till tomorrow when you'll see your son covered in blood. That'll set your ideas straight as we're in a situation of rising violence. Good night, Kisses.

Day 18

The Martin Durand Case

The detectives are worn out. The kidnapper's evident cruelty, the technical difficulties his movements create, as well as last week's failed trap, show them just how helpless they are. As for the ongoing investigations, they don't seem to lead anywhere. Not one witness has been able to identify any of the lures, and the anonymous information sent to the Quai des Orfèvres are yet more imaginings. And, so far, the wanted poster hasn't led anywhere either.

The Anti-Crime Brigade detectives have run out of ideas, when a letter of request gives them permission to investigate the violence perpetrated against Martin Durand on January 6 at Arcueil. Just this morning, on the theory that the people who attacked this man may be the same as those who have my son, the magistrate in Créteil handed the case over to the Anti-Crime Brigade. Armed with this letter of request, the Quai des Orfèvres immediately summons Durand, his son Jacques, as well as

Frederic Arnaud, the friend who's staying with them and who let the lure into the apartment. Durand recounts his meeting with Melvina, the so-called singer. He describes her as a young girl with Slavic features, twenty to twenty-two years old, about five foot four, and of very slight build. He adds that she has bangs, dark, shoulder-length, straight hair, and that her blue eyes are slightly slanted. He remembers that she had an accent from an Eastern European country, but she told him she was from Arles. So Melvina is nothing like Lea, the girl who tried to seduce Maurice Keller, the cell-phone salesman, and even less like the brunette with North African features who led Ilan into the trap.

The police deduce that there's a third lure involved in this affair. And they're right. Later, they discover that in an attempt to make it even more difficult to trace them, the criminals had recruited the third girl in Marseille.

Arnaud, who is questioned as a witness, adds a few interesting details: Melvina told him she was a beautician—Lea also claimed to work in that field—and that she sometimes worked as a stripper to make some extra money.

This last bit of information convinces the investigators that the Hustler, a nightclub known for this type of show, and that's come up several times during the investigation, could lead to the criminals.

In fact, before falling back on boulevard Voltaire, where Ilan was targeted, the criminal had sent a lure and two of his accomplices to the Hustler on December 29, with a view toward picking up phone numbers. That's how Melvina had obtained Jean Loiselle's number and had called him, introducing herself as Natacha. But, since the ringleader had the feeling this guy wasn't Jewish, he finally told her to forget him and chose to focus on the Sentier and the boulevard Voltaire areas instead, in order to increase his chances of finding a victim who fitted his bill: a Jew.

At the Quai des Orfèvres, Durand and Arnaud tell investigators that they've never been to the Hustler. Jacques, Durand's son, expresses certain suspicions about Renée, one of his ex-girlfriends, who's now going out with a bouncer she met at the Hustler, so the investigators show them the 150 photos of women photographed there by the Anti-Pimping Brigade. Jacques thinks this girl may have met Melvina at the nightclub, since Melvina had told Arnaud that she sometimes worked as a stripper. Maybe Melvina told Renée she wanted to become a singer, and Renée suggested that Melvina get in touch with her ex-boyfriend, a music producer named Jacques Durand.

March 12, 2016

NEWTON, Mass.—Parents and students at a championship basketball game between Newton North High and Catholic Memorial High were shocked when Catholic Memorial fans started shouting, "You killed Jesus!" The chant was presumably aimed at Newton High's sizable Jewish student population. "I found it chilling," Newton superintendent David Fleishman told the *Boston Globe*. Although the students involved eventually apologized, the incident left Newton basketball captain Nate Hollenberg shaken. "They might not have meant it so personally, but you should think about things before you speak," he told the *Globe*. "That hurts. They're coming at my religion, at who I am, a big part of me. That's just not right."

Day 19

Blind Alleys

Renée Jouer is brought into police custody. But, after checking the information she provides, they soon think she has nothing to do with the case.

As for Martin Durand and Frederic Arnaud, they can't identify Melvina from any of the photos they're shown. They will recognize her a few days later, however, from the same series of photographs, but by then it's too late.

Apart from Renée, Jacques Durand suspects a singer who had come to see him when he was still a record producer. The investigators take this intuition seriously, since the artist he mentions is a rapper. Earlier, the Quai des Orfèvres had received a letter implicating a rapper, and the kidnapper was filmed in the internet café wearing an Adedi sweatshirt, a brand favored by the urban music world.

Durand no longer has this musician's contact information, and the Anti-Crime Brigade takes ages to track him down. The musician's testimony will turn out to be crucial . . . In fact, when he makes his statement at the beginning of March, the rapper admits that he'd been to Durand's home a few months earlier with Jérémy Pastisson, "a friend from Bagneux." And he remembers that Jérémy had been very interested in everything and very excited about Durand's comfortable lifestyle. So excited that, once he was back in Bagneux, Jérémy told his friends about the evening he'd spent at a "rich Jewish producer's place." That day, Youssouf Fofana was among those listening, and he listened well . . . He asks for the name and address of this man who would make a perfect victim, then decides to send a girl there. That's how, on January 5, Melvina, passing herself off as a singer, went to the Durand residence.

I am to learn one day that Jérémy, who found Jacques Durand, was also involved in Ilan's ordeal: It was his vehicle that was used to kidnap my son from the "green alley" in Sceaux and take him to the place where he was imprisoned, the apartment on rue Serge Prokofiev in Bagneux.

✦

The phone number for Melvina that Durand gives to the police is not in service. Nonetheless, a close examination of the contacts on his cell phone allows the Anti-Crime Brigade to identify two other possible suspects: Orville Aubert and Jaimie Garnier. The former, already known to the police, has just been released from prison. He's immediately suspected of being involved in the attack on Martin Durand. So he's also brought to the Quai des Orfèvres.

But like Maurice Keller, the cell-phone salesman, Aubert is actually a victim. A member of the Jewish faith, he has also escaped a kidnapping attempt. He tells the investigators his story.

At the end of 2005 he received a call on his cell from a young girl who said she wanted to meet him. As was the case with the Durands, she introduces herself as Melvina and claims to have gotten his number from a friend they have in common, whose name she refuses to disclose. She claims to fancy him, and flatters him, praising his good looks; she's quite a minx. Aubert isn't taken in. He has the feeling there's something wrong, and he thinks it's a prank his girlfriend has set up to see if he's really faithful to her. Nonetheless, out of curiosity, he sends his friend Garnier to the meeting arranged by Melvina. The young people go to a café, while Aubert drives around on his scooter to check that no one's trying to trap him. Eventually, he goes back to the bistro. When he finally introduces himself, he notes Melvina's look of surprise. But she is supposed to have known him . . . Aubert tries to get her to tell him where she got his phone number, but Melvina's not giving anything away, so Aubert decides to leave. And Garnier takes advantage of his friend's departure to suggest to the girl that they get better acquainted. Melvina pretends to be charmed by him.

Days later, she tells Garnier to meet her in the same place she had met Martin Durand, in front of the Arcueil train station, at about 9:00 p.m. She gets there a few minutes late and they exchange a few pleasantries, then she invites him back to her place, claiming she has to pick up some of her things. When they reach her building, she tries very hard to make Garnier take the ramp to the parking area in the basement. The young man is very uneasy. He doesn't think Melvina actually lives here, since she's so awkward. And then he can't understand why she's so intent on his walking through the basement of this building in the middle of the night. "I'll wait for you here," he tells her, and he lets her go off into the basement alone. He uses this opportunity to call Aubert, and he tells his friend how strangely Melvina is behaving.

Aubert advises him not to take any risks and to get out of there immediately. Garnier follows his advice.

Once he's back home, he calls Melvina to apologize for disappearing so suddenly. He's chatting with her calmly, when suddenly a man grabs the phone from Melvina to tell him he's just escaped a trap intended for Aubert.

Garnier immediately tells his friend. They set up a phone meeting between the victim and the criminal. The criminal warns Aubert that there's a contract out on his life, and, despite this evening's mess-up, it will soon be carried out. In other words, he tells him he's going to be killed. He adds that he's willing to tell him who's behind it, but it'll cost him 30,000 euros. Aubert doesn't take the threat seriously, and he jokes about it, but the man's final words worry him: The criminal knows his mother's address and his brother's name. Aubert doesn't press charges at the time. Does this reflect carelessness, a lack of a civic sense, a desire to stay away from the police after his recent sojourn in prison? Whatever the reasons that motivated his decision . . . Two months later the kidnappers have fine-tuned their sinister enterprise. They "tested" it on Martin Durand and Maurice Keller, learning something from these failed kidnap attempts, and used these lessons to improve their plan, setting the trap Ilan walked into. Today Aubert thinks he can rightly say that the person on the phone was African, and, from his accent, it seemed he was from the slums. Aubert noticed his limited vocabulary, his jerky speech, so many details that tally with the characteristics of the language used by Ilan's kidnapper. But how can we catch this man? The investigators question Aubert: Is there anyone in particular he suspects? Who could have it in for him to the point of wanting to kidnap him? Is he involved in drug deals or gambling? Does he owe anyone money? "I have no enemies. I haven't bullshitted anyone. I haven't conned anyone," states Aubert confidently. He's lying. The investigators tell him that Ilan has been kidnapped, that he has been imprisoned for eighteen days, so I believe he knows his answers could save Ilan's life, but he lies.

Aubert has enemies. When he was released from prison, he borrowed money from Karl Fouad from Bagneux, one of the prisoners with whom he shared a cell. Aubert promised to pay him back quickly, but he didn't keep his word, and the creditor keeps asking for his money.

Why doesn't Aubert mention this disagreement? Why doesn't he say that just after he escaped the trap he contacted his creditor, as he had the feeling Fouad knew the people who had attacked him? The kidnapping attempt had taken place at Arcueil; Fouad lived in Bagneux. He must have known them. I feel that if Aubert hadn't been so concerned about his own interests, if he'd set aside his ongoing petty disagreements with this guy, he would have admitted to being in debt and shared the creditor's identity while there was still time to act. He would only bring it up at the end of June. He waited until he'd made three statements before he gave them the identity of the creditor who had targeted him. We are to discover later that Fouad, who was fed up with waiting for his money, had asked Youssouf Fofana to lean on Aubert.

Once again the Anti-Crime Brigade had come within an inch of identifying the criminal and saving my son. If only Aubert had given them a name, just one name, Karl Fouad, the criminal enterprise would have been dismantled . . . What can I say but that life is a question of luck.

Ilan's had run out.

August 11–12, 2017

CHARLOTTESVILLE, VA.—For two days this college town rang with racist, anti-Semitic chants, as white supremacists gathered to make their bigotry known publicly. Adorned in swastikas and carrying Confederate flags, the marchers shouted, "Jews will not replace us!" Late Saturday afternoon, white supremacist James Fields Jr. drove his car into a crowd of antiracist protesters, killing activist Heather Heyer. Victims cried out in pain while onlookers howled in shock and ran from the scene, shouting for medical help. "Oh, my God," someone screamed, according to Los Angeles Times reports. "He mowed down everybody."

Day 20

The Last Email

We receive one final email from the kidnapper:

> We're beginning to think you don't want to pay. If I don't get the money we plan to kill him.

Martin Durand is summoned to the Quai des Orfèvres again. Of all the victims, he's the only one who was physically assaulted. He passed out, he doesn't remember anything, but he spent two consecutive evenings with Melvina, one of the lures. And, above all, the day before he was attacked in Arcueil, he had dropped her at Bagneux. The detectives want to go there. So Durand takes them to the main road that separates the neighborhoods of Montrouge and Bagneux; he tells them to stop near a car wash. He remembers that he had left the girl in front of this sign. She had then walked toward the group of redbrick buildings, but he can't say precisely which one she'd gone into, since he hadn't hung around.

The last time Ilan's cell phone had pinged, it was off a cell tower in Sceaux. The attempts to kidnap Durand and Orville Aubert both took place in Arcueil. As for the kidnapper's calls and emails, most of them came from the Fourteenth Arrondissement, the closest Parisian neighborhood to these suburbs in the Ile de France region. The investigators have a strong feeling that in Bagneux they can't be far from where this gang of criminals gathers. They're right. Avenue Henri Ravera, the long main road running alongside the Parisian cemetery in Bagneux, down which Durand brought them, is only a few hundred yards from rue Serge Prokofiev, where Ilan is being held prisoner. From the car wash, you just have to go three hundred yards up avenue Henri Ravera, toward Paris, turn right onto rue Jean Marin Naudin, and cross the small rue de Turin.

The detectives are a five-minute walk from where he's being held. Just a five-minute walk . . . Since they have no leads, they decide to talk to the concierge of the building opposite the car wash. It's not an easy job: If the criminals are operating in the area, the police have to be very discreet.

The Anti-Crime Brigade asks for a list of all the building's tenants, and their identities are closely examined, but nothing jumps out at the authorities. In addition, the photo of Fofana, and Lea and Melvina's identikit photos, are shown to the female concierge. Although she has no idea who the African-looking guy is, she clearly identifies Melvina as the live-in girlfriend of one of the tenants, who's known to the police. This information is treated as a serious clue, yet after checking it out, it turns out that the girl in question has nothing to do with the case. Just like the former tenant whom the concierge thinks is Lea . . .

The investigation in Bagneux doesn't lead anywhere. And although the investigators were careful and very discreet in order to avoid compromising the negotiations, yet again, their superiors bring this new initiative to a halt. The kidnapper is in such a rage, his crazed words are so unbearable, that there's no room for discussion.

The Research and Intervention Brigade and the psychologists can no longer control Didier. Ilan's father has had enough. He's received over six hundred phone calls in three weeks, sometimes up to twenty a day; he's a mere shadow of his former self. Given the nervous tension that's built up, the Quai des Orfèvres would like him to take a break. The chief inspector convinces us that this is the right thing to do, reminding us that every time the kidnapper breaks off communication, he's always contacted us again via the internet. If he were to do this again, we'd have a chance of locating him. The police hope they'll get another lucky break. How many have they had already? How many times have they let the opportunity of saving my son slip away? Didier, however, continues to trust them. In any event, he has no choice. The kidnapper is mad with rage, and the horror of his words makes us nauseous:

"So in what state do you want him back?" he asks Didier in a message left on his voice mail. "You'll get him back six feet under. And I'm warning you now, you know what you should do? Take your sperm and spread it over the bank notes, that'll give you a new child, fucking dog . . ."

Day 21

Waiting

Day 22

Waiting

Day 23

Waiting

Day 24

Naked and Alone

What Are We Waiting For?

Eve marches up and down the corridor. She moves methodically, never breaking stride, her face twisted in a rage that I think will soon erupt. She could overturn the clothes closets or harm herself. I've never seen such anger in my daughter's face. It's the silence that's killing her. And the investigators' waiting, which she sees as a cop-out. "What are they waiting for?" she repeats over and over from between clenched teeth. Ilan's been held hostage for three weeks now. It's Monday, February 13, and we've had no news for four days. Not a single call. Not a single email. The kidnapper has never been silent for such a long time.

We're so tense that this morning Eve ends up fighting with her father on the phone. She screams at him, as if it were his fault. What are you waiting for—to make contact with them again? In her fury I catch a glimpse of the little girl who used to say,

"My dad's the strongest." Why wasn't he strong anymore? Why couldn't he save Ilan? Despite being twenty-five years old, Eve couldn't understand. But what could Didier do . . .?

"We have to listen to the police. We have to trust them; they know what they're doing," he replies.

He doesn't fully believe his own words—you can hear it in his voice. There has been too much violence and too many suppressed tears for it to be true. I suppose he just wants to protect his daughter: It is so awful to watch our other children suffer.

"They're going to kill him!" shouts Eve.

She needs to shake her father up. If he'd been her son, she would have slapped him; he was the only one she could take her anger out on. And too bad if it hurt him, too bad if he didn't deserve her fury after the three nightmarish weeks he'd just endured. She knew it was the end. Since the previous day, she'd heard me saying it over and over again.

I knew immediately that I'd never see my son again. I'd realized that on the second day he'd been missing, at the Quai des Orfèvres, as I stood before the large wall covered in photographs of people who had disappeared. They were like hundreds of black cats, all these photos displayed on the wall, like signs being sent to warn me. But to whom could I have said it? I kept quiet; I pretended to believe. And over time, a small ray of hope emerged, like an ember that hasn't quite gone out. So I blew on it, I repeated absurd incantations that we use to ward off misfortune: It's the bad guys who are punished. I'm not bad. I've never killed anyone, never stolen anything, never harmed anyone, something like this can't be happening to me. Last night, while I was asleep, I realized it could.

Mothers Know Everything

I had just fallen asleep when I felt an incredible force pick my bed up and hurl it against the wall. It was more violent than a car accident. I didn't feel it coming. It was as if the elements had gone wild and were trying to destroy my room. Or rather my life.

I woke up suffocating. I went to see the two cops who were awake in the living room, and I said to them: "Something's happened to Ilan." Obviously, they didn't believe me. They thought, Poor woman, with all that she's going through, it's normal for her to have nightmares. But I knew this wasn't a nightmare. Yes, I knew the worst had befallen us, and not just in my dreams. A cataclysm of that magnitude couldn't be brought on by my imagination.

I went back to bed, and, behind my closed eyes, the same scene played itself out again. My bed hurled against the wall with a resounding bang, my bedroom smashed to bits, my life fragmented. I think it was my own cries that woke me. It was five in the morning.

They say a mother knows everything, and this is how I know it's true. Today, at 5:00 a.m., Ilan's torturer dumps him in the woods. He would gladly have prolonged Ilan's ordeal, but his accomplices had had enough of being jailers. They realized there wasn't a cent coming their way, and they wanted out. Abandoned by his lieutenants, the ringleader had no choice but to agree.

He orders them to wash the Jew and to shave his head, precisely because he is Jewish and he has to come to the same end as so many other Jews before him. Washed and shaven, to be led to his death. His torturers carry out these instructions, taking the same pleasure in following orders as the barbarians of yesterday. They shave my son's head with disposable razors, and his lovely black hair is scattered over the basement floor, as the hair of six million innocents was sacrificed before.

Just as the Einsatzgruppen assassinated Eastern European Jews outside their towns, Ilan is transported to the small woods in the trunk of a car. He is taken to the small grove that marks the border between the suburbs of Sainte-Geneviève-des-Bois and Villemoisson-sur-Orge. The kidnapper chooses to dump him there, naked, in the dark, freezing night, when he notices Ilan has removed the blindfold that obscures his view. My son is looking him right in the eye. My son knows he is going to die, but he defies him in order to state he is a Man. I am a Man, his eyes say. You tried to turn me into an animal, but you failed. I will remain a Man till my last breath. He is stabbed several times in the throat and the sides, but none of the wounds is fatal. So the torturer keeps going. He pours gasoline over him and sets him on fire.

Ilan is a Jew; he has to go up in smoke.

Along the Train Track

It's a rainy Monday morning, the kind of Monday in February you'd rather spend in bed than in your car, but Pauline Girard has to get to work. She's driving her Citroën. She's a secretary, like me. I have no idea whether she's married, whether she has children. All I know is she's a young, thirty-eight-year-old French woman, who travels this route daily from Longpont to Sainte-Geneviève-des-Bois to get to her office. So on this terribly familiar journey, as the windshield wipers swish away the unceasing rain, I imagine her thinking of the sunshine in her homeland, Cameroon, of what she'd done the evening before, or what she'd do tomorrow evening, or her shopping, or her washing. I imagine she is lost in her own thoughts when, to her right, just before the sign indicating the entrance to the town of Villemoisson-sur-Orge, she glimpses a shape that looks like a body. For a moment she thinks she's imagining things; she's driving at thirty miles an hour, maybe she hasn't really seen what it is . . . What she sees is so shocking that she looks again to make sure, and it is indeed a human being that she can make out, lying beside the railroad track. The man—or the woman, she doesn't know which—seems to be naked and immobile. Girard doesn't wait to reach her office; she immediately calls the police from her cell phone.

Thanks to this driver's phone call, Ilan is found at 8:55 a.m., by two police constables—a man and a very young female trainee, barely older than my son. They find Ilan naked, handcuffed, burns over his entire body, leaning against the fence that keeps people off the train tracks. The fencing is too high for them to climb over, so they have to walk some way until they find a place low enough for them to cross and then return to Ilan on the other side. When they reach him, they see that there is tape around his forehead and his neck. They see that in addition to being covered in bruises and burns, he has wounds to his Achilles tendon and neck. There is a hole in his throat.

Ilan is still breathing. Weakly, but he is breathing. The flames haven't killed him. He's tried to live. After the hell of being locked away, after the fear, the cold, the hunger, and the pain, after being slashed with a box cutter and a knife, after his body has caught fire like a torch, there had also been the calvary of the "last walk" . . . The ordeal thousands of other Jews have been subjected to before him.

The constable climbs onto the track to inspect the site. The young trainee remains beside my son. She stays with him until the emergency services arrive at 9:15. He is still alive, and maybe he can hear. Yes, that's what I keep telling myself in order not to go mad. Ilan doesn't die like a dog. He hears this girl's voice before he dies, a gentle, kind voice. That's all I have to comfort me.

His heart stops several times, then it stops beating completely, and he is declared dead at midday at Cochin Hospital. "X died," the doctor writes, because, at the time, no one knows who he is. It is only the photographs taken by the Versailles Anti-Crime Brigade, when he was in the ambulance, that lead to his being identified. I imagine these photos were sent the same day to the various police departments... Although this doesn't actually seem to have been the case, since, when I went to the Quai des Orfèvres that day, at 6:30 p.m., to beg the chief inspector to make contact with the kidnappers again, no one told me my son was dead. No one tells me a young man has been found beside a train track at Sainte-Geneviève-des-Bois. I only hear about it the following day, alone in my office, when I read the human-interest section of the paper *20 Minutes*. I call the chief inspector myself to ask him to confirm my premonition, to hear from him that this "man" in the daily paper is indeed my son.

The chief inspector doesn't want to say anything over the phone. He doesn't come to see me, either. Instead, he sends a terribly young policewoman, pale and trembling, who mumbles: "I'm sorry, Madam, I can't tell you anything." She drives me to the Quai des Orfèvres, then takes me up to the fourth floor. Didier is already in the chief inspector's office. He is seated, looking out onto the Seine. I can see his profile, and his tears speak volumes.

2016 and ongoing

NATIONWIDE, USA—"Look around, white man. Take your country back!" So said the flier posted online by the white supremacist group Vanguard America.

American college students and administrators report a rising tide of anti-Semitic, racist, and anti-immigrant fliers appearing on campuses across the country, as white supremacists target students as part of a concerted effort to attract younger followers and raise their collective profile. From Boston, to Washington, D.C., to Los Angeles, students are struggling with how to respond. Student activists at the University of Massachusetts in Boston were divided on the issue: Katharine O'Donnell told an NPR reporter she didn't want to give the white supremacists any more attention, but fellow student Gabriella Cartagena disagreed. "We have to let people know that this is not okay," she told NPR. "We have to do something about this. We can't just push it under the rug."

The Immediate Aftermath

Monique Joly reaches work early. She settles into the break room while she waits for the shop where she works as a salesgirl to open. She makes herself a cup of coffee. She unfolds her copy of *20 Minutes,* dated February 15. She hasn't watched the news or read the papers for a few days. She is flipping through the news, not looking for anything in particular, when suddenly an identikit photo of a young, blond girl jumps out at her. It's Audrey Lorleach, her friend; she recognizes her immediately. What's she doing in the newspaper? Why are they looking for her?

Because she led a boy into a trap, says the article. Because this boy was imprisoned and tortured for three weeks. Because he was found dead and the criminals are still at large.

If Joly had any doubt about whether this was her friend Lorleach, she's now convinced that it is, because at the beginning of January, Lorleach had told her that she was going to be paid 5,000 euros to chat up a Jew and get his phone number. Then, she was supposed to call him and set up a meeting so she could take him somewhere where he'd be attacked. The Jew would be kidnapped, she'd pretend she escaped, and she'd get her money.

Joly disapproved of the scheme. She had threatened to tell Lorleach's parents, but Lorleach had gotten mad at her, and the discussion had ended there. A few days later, Lorleach, who'd obtained the number of a certain Maurice Keller, told Joly that she didn't have "the guts" to follow through with this criminal act. Nonetheless, she confessed, "the criminals" had found another lure to seduce another Jew. And this other Jew is in an empty apartment in Pierre-Plate, in Bagneux . . .

From the beginning Joly knew Ilan had been imprisoned, but she didn't say a word to anyone.

What should she do now that the press was involved? Call Lorleach's parents? The police? Her friend? In the early afternoon, she decides to send Lorleach a text message: "I'm coming round this evening, its urgent," she writes, as if there were still time to lecture her.

Lorleach cries. She says her face is in every newspaper; she's in "deep shit." She knows that sooner or later someone will catch her. So, on her friend Joly's advice, she decides to go to the police station in Montrouge of her own free will.

✦

The police discover that the girl they know as "Lea," the young, shapely blonde, is the one who went into a cell phone store on boulevard Voltaire and got Maurice Keller's phone number. The Quai des Orfèvres had prepared the identikit photo of this girl at the end of January, but, thinking it would endanger Ilan's life, they had decided not to publish it.

For my part, I think, on the contrary, this could have saved him. Yes, I think that if the media had been informed, if these identikit photos and the photo of my son had been broadcast by every means possible, Ilan would have survived. That was the investigators' first major mistake. And, in fact, two weeks after Ilan's death, the attorney general decided to make some changes: He signed the "Kidnapping Alert" agreement for children.

Within three hours of a child's disappearance this plan allows the kidnapped child's photograph and description to be broadcast on all the television channels and radio stations, as well as on all the display panels in train stations, metro stations, on motorways, and in airports. My son's death led to the adoption of this emergency measure . . . But he wouldn't have been able to benefit from it anyway. He was twenty-three, and this plan is applicable only to minors.

October 27, 2018

PITTSBURGH—At 9:50 a.m., in the midst of Saturday services, Robert Bowers, armed with an assault rifle and three handguns, burst into the Tree of Life Synagogue in Pittsburgh's Squirrel Hill neighborhood shouting, "All Jews must die!" He opened fire. Rabbi Jeffrey Myers, who fled to the bathroom in the choir loft after helping several congregants escape, dialed 911 as quietly as he could.

First responders arrived on the scene in minutes and ran toward the gunfire into the synagogue. But by the time the shooter was apprehended, eleven people, all longtime Tree of Life members, were dead. Six people, including four police officers, were wounded. "This is the most horrific crime scene I've seen in twenty-two years," a veteran FBI agent said at an afternoon press conference. The shooter, who called Jews the "children of Satan," blamed Jewish international aid work for an "invasion" of immigrants and refugees.

Postscript

Confessions

At the Montrouge police station, Lea admits that her real name is Audrey Lorleach, she did try to lead Maurice Keller into a trap, but in Ilan's case, it was another girl who served as the lure. And she gives them the name of her boyfriend, Jérôme Ribeiro, who had told her he was one of the jailers.

On Thursday, February 16, this young man is arrested and ordered to name his accomplices. Armed with his confession, that night, about two hundred policemen enter the buildings of the Pierre-Plate housing project: Pierre Plate, Prunier Hardy, and Tilleul in Bagneux. Thirteen people suspected of being involved in Ilan's ordeal are arrested. All of them blame everything on a single man they say is the undisputed mastermind behind this sinister plan: Youssouf Fofana.

Youssouf Fofana's arrest

What risks does a "ringleader" run when he's left the country? Youssouf Fofana had flown off to Ivory Coast again, two days after killing Ilan. The investigators locate him in Abidjan, thanks to the insulting messages he leaves on his lieutenants' cell phones. The man is enraged. He's read the French press online, and he knows he's been denounced as the chief culprit.

His face is on the front page of every newspaper; he's public enemy number one. But that doesn't force him into hiding; in fact, quite the opposite. He continues to come and go freely in the suburbs of Abidjan as if he has nothing to fear, as if Ivory Coast police can't arrest him. At the motel where he's staying, he registers under his real name and invites his girlfriend to spend the night with him. "Usually, he came in in the night, his hands thrust into his pockets," the receptionist confides to *Paris Match*. "Then he would spend all morning in his room. He would go out at midday, on foot. . . . He behaved like someone serene, at least outwardly, someone who had nothing to hide."

Yes, it seems Youssouf Fofana thinks he is above the law, all-powerful, and this feeling of impunity allows him to continue to harass us. On Thursday, February 16, he calls Didier on his cell phone to ask him if he is happy. That day Didier is in his car on his way to the morgue . . . And the next morning, as we are getting ready to bury my son, Youssouf Fofana calls Mony, Ilan's girlfriend, to threaten her; she is to be his next victim.

✦

The magistrate issues an international arrest warrant for Youssouf Fofana, and Ivory Coast police are informed of his presence in their territory. Despite the tension between the two countries, officials in Ivory Coast behave perfectly: They assure France that they will cooperate fully and set up a large-scale operation to arrest the fugitive. We fear he will move into the rebel areas, and if he does that we know there will be next to no chance of finding him.

Against all odds, on February 22, at about 9:00 p.m., one of Youssouf Fofana's cousins calls the police station in Abidjan's Fifteenth Arrondissement to inform police that the suspect is in a white Toyota in the Abobo area. The capital's police chief orders his troops to cover the area and leads the operation himself. At 10:15 p.m. the vehicle in question is seen at a traffic circle: It only takes a policeman's whistle to stop it.

Handcuffed immediately, the person who admits that his name is Youssouf Fofana is taken to police headquarters. He doesn't seem to understand why he's been arrested until he's introduced to the two French policemen who had arrived in Abidjan the previous day.

"What do you want with me, you dogs?" he says to them.

"We're here to take you back to France, where you're wanted for murder."

Youssouf Fofana then claims to be a jihadist and an Islamist. He admits to ordering Ilan's kidnapping and unabashedly states that he has deliberately chosen a Jew. Even if he later denies the anti-Semitic nature of his criminal act, I know he speaks the truth: He targeted a man because of that man's religious belief.

✦

On March 2, 2006, Laurent Gbagbo, president of Ivory Coast, signs the extradition decree for Youssouf Fofana. Two days later, he is brought back to Paris and placed in temporary detention. Like all the other accused, he is held accountable for his actions before the French courts.

In all, twenty-nine suspects were taken into custody for "associating with criminals, kidnapping, holding somebody against his or her will as an organized gang, acts of torture and barbarism and assassination." The court took into account the aggravating circumstances of acts committed "due to the victim's belonging to a specific ethnic group, race or religion."

Fofana was sentenced to life in prison with no possibility of parole for twenty-two years. His two most active accomplices received sentences of up to eighteen years in prison. Others involved in the crime were sentenced to between six months and nine years in prison. Two defendants were acquitted.

Mourning

I am no more than a shadow of my former self. A zombie. A ghost. I remain cloistered in my apartment, as required by tradition, immobile in a corner of my living room, praying, to avoid going mad. Time has stopped. Every day is night.

In the week since Ilan's funeral, my apartment has never been empty. People line up on the staircase to offer their condolences. Some cry. Others take my hand. Most of them don't know what to say. But is there anything they could say?

The journalists lie in wait outside the building. They want to know if the rumors are true, if Ilan was kidnapped because he was Jewish. Everything points in that direction—the statements made by the gang's other victims, the information revealed by the lures, the torturers' confessions—everything except the district attorney's statements: He keeps repeating that the motive behind the crime is purely financial. So? Where does the truth lie?

Maurice Keller, Martin and Jacques Durand, Orville Aubert,

Jaimie Garnier, the names of the Jewish men who escaped the trap by the skin of their teeth, go round and round in my head. The messages left for the rabbi hammer away at my brain—a Jew has been kidnapped, a Jew is being held prisoner—and Ilan's voice on the cassettes—"I'm a Jew, I'm being held prisoner."

I hold my peace for three weeks. I did as the police asked and my son died. Should I still do as they say? Should I allow the district attorney to make his statements despite everything I know? Out of respect for the ordeal my son endured I can't, and for this reason, in the midst of my mourning, I decide to speak out on RTL radio, to state what the district attorney refuses to:

> Ilan was chosen because he was Jewish. They attacked him persistently. They lynched him. While he was alive, they burned him, they cut him just because he was Jewish. If Ilan hadn't been a Jew, he wouldn't have been killed.

✦

The magistrates in charge of the case add anti-Semitism as an aggravating factor. This decision won't bring back my son, but it's a huge relief—the proof that France still respects its ideals of justice.

After the desecration of Jewish graves and a body in Carpentras in 1990, tens of thousands of people come out into the streets in protest. Jews, Muslims, Catholics, the blacks-blancs-beurs demonstrated arm in arm, proudly showing off the Stars of David pinned to the lapels of their jackets. Today, the French haven't changed, they haven't become less sensitive or less human—the hundreds of letters I received are proof of this.

The sorrow of having lost my son is compounded by the pain of seeing an abhorrent debate emerge. Mere prejudice, stupidity, ignorance, a financial crime, some said, despite the anti-Semitic statements made by the chief suspect, whose words were reported in all the newspapers. This obstinate refusal to look reality in the face wounds me, offends me, revolts me. It makes me feel as if Ilan were dying a second time; denying the reasons for his ordeal was like killing him all over again.

But to bring me some peace, there were French people of all faiths, of all colors, of all descents. French people who, in another time, would have supported Dreyfus, or would have joined the Resistance movement, and who won't let anti-Semitism disfigure our country again. These French people told me of their shame, their hatred, their indignation, sent me hundreds of letters and emails, and I would like them to know how much their words comforted me. I want to share a few excerpts of these letters, proving that my son wasn't wrong: Ilan deeply believed in the goodness of humankind.

Excerpts from the Letters of Support: Such Kind Words

> I'm a Catholic. When I heard this terrible news, I felt like a Jew. Dear Madam, please know that the heart of every mother worthy of this title, of every single faith, bleeds for you.
>
> —*Pascale*

> A simple letter, one of so many . . . I don't know what words to use to express our unbearable pain . . . Know that we have all lost a brother, a son . . . Ilan paid for our community, he was sacrificed . . . I would like

to help you find the courage to transform this pain into strength. Into the strength to keep Ilan alive, to perpetuate his memory, to make sure these monsters, who wanted to destroy you, don't win.

—*Virginie*

In the name of my family and all those who believe in humanity

Who believe in God

I ask your forgiveness, once, twice, three times over

May reason triumph, triumph on every front

May hearts be at peace and passions calmed

May human beings come out of this greater, may they learn from this

My words won't bring Ilan back, they won't revive his flame

But if, even for an instant, if they can calm your soul

I would be so happy, so proud

And even if our beliefs are different

May his memory live on in both our souls, in both our prayers.

—*Mohammed*

Ilan,

I'm a young actress, a theater director and a writer, yet I can't find the words. I can't find the words to describe the pain you suffered. So I just want to promise you something: As long as the world exists, you'll never be forgotten. Because there will always be millions of us to shout, to scream our remembrance! From my stage, I'll never forget to leave room for you beside me, in the name of your family, in the name of every Jew who was exterminated, in the name of peace. And together, all together, we'll fight so that history won't repeat itself.

—Caroline

While Ilan was going through this drama I learned that I was expecting a baby. I was deeply affected by these terrible events. I had a little girl, but if I'd had a little boy, his name would have been Ilan. My thoughts often turn to Ilan and his family. Stand firm.

—Carole

I only learned of this story from the press. I'm not Jewish; I'm Catholic. I'm neither a believer, nor do I practice a religion, but what happened to Ilan touched something deep within me.

I wish you all the happiness you deserve. Kisses.

—Anne-Sophie

Ilan, I cried sincere tears for you. I attended your funeral on the television and I felt a terrible sadness within me . . . as if I were burying a member of my own family . . . I belong to a Muslim family but how does religion matter, as no human being deserves to suffer what you did.

Ilan, we cry for you and ask you to forgive us.

We ask the Halimi family to forgive us, as we are all

guilty. We need to protect our cousins, the Jews, to be as close to them as Prophet Muhammad was.

—Mourad

I don't believe in any religion, but as a human being, like so many others I was touched and revolted by this barbarian murder, by how widespread anti-Semitic clichés are, by the murderous stupidity, the spinelessness and cowardice of all those (thirty people of all kinds of descent!) who organized and participated, to varying degrees, in the kidnapping, imprisonment, and murder of Ilan Halimi.

—Zonek

Know that it is not only Jews who are touched by this terrible crime, but so many French people of every faith. I'm a Catholic myself, and today, New Year's Eve, I send all of you loving thoughts and prayers for peace and compassion.

—Patricia

Madame Halimi, I was pregnant with my son when your beloved left you. I called my son Ilan in homage to yours. I was told that in Hebrew, it means little tree. Even though I'm Muslim, I wanted to show that even if the leaves are torn off, the trunk remains.

—Ylan

My God, people have gone mad . . . Why so much hatred?

Your story touched all of us . . . It's inhuman, unfair, and horrible; there are no words to describe it.

Ilan, may your memory rest in peace forever. Let us fight so that something like this never happens again.

We're thinking of the Halimi family. We're with you in our hearts.

From a Christian who loves you . . . to the Jews

—Muriel

A thought for Ilan, the young man who didn't deserve this. I am horrified to see that such acts were committed against an innocent person . . . I'm a practicing Muslim, and I strongly condemn this barbarism. We should be tolerant toward every community. It's up to us to set an example and to live in peace with everyone, to respect people's origins.

Rest in peace.

—Malika

I'm hurting for our humanity that's deteriorating every year. Ilan, to us you'll always be the symbol of a joie de vivre that was annihilated! Today I'm sad for your family, everyone close to you, and the Jewish people as a whole. I will name one of my children after you so that you'll continue to live among us.

Amen.

—Thomas

The Final Journey

THE FEBRUARY SUNSHINE illuminates Jerusalem. I'm told it rained all week, but I find that difficult to believe, as the weather is wonderful today. It warms my heart. Although I'm not really at home here, today, in particular, I feel as if I've come home. Yes, I feel like a young adult who's come back to her parents' home, seeking comfort.

The Givat Shaul Cemetery in western Jerusalem is a vast, immaculate park. Perched on a hilltop overlooking the town, it lies amid trees that are hundreds of years old. It's steeped in silence, interrupted only by the sound of the wind. And sometimes birdsong. The white alleys and tombs, on which the living come to leave milky stones, stretch far into the distance under a sky that's so blue you'd think it's the sea. Here there are no funerary monuments like those you find in our cemeteries, just simple rectangles; their sobriety almost makes you forget you're among the dead.

We arrived from Paris early this morning, with my son-in-law David and my two daughters. Deborah stayed behind at the hotel. She can't attend her brother's funeral as she's pregnant. She's carrying a new life, so she mustn't approach the dead. Ilan's father isn't here, either. I think he didn't have the strength to face yet another ordeal. But I'm not alone. My family and close friends are with me. I'm surrounded by my brothers, who live here.

I recognize a few faces in the crowd gathered in the mourning room, although most are unknown to me. Later I'm told that over five hundred anonymous visitors came from all over the country, and even from France, to accompany Ilan to his final resting place. I would like to thank them, but I can barely look at them. They're young and handsome and full of life. It's even more difficult to see them, all gathered here, than it is to know my son is lying in a shroud at my feet. Following the tradition, he's been taken out of his casket and wrapped in a simple white sheet. That's how we bury our dead.

So, Ilan is lying here on the ground, wrapped in this cloth. Beneath it you can make out his head, his torso, his legs. It's the first time I'm seeing my son again since Friday, January 20, 2006, the day he was kidnapped. I didn't go to the morgue to identify his body. His father went. I just couldn't.

Jean-Michel Casa, the French ambassador to Israel, makes a speech: "Ilan was a young man, full of life, energy, and joy, and in his death he has come to represent all men, in the very name of this obligation bestowed upon each of us, to respect life."

His life—I see it play across his shroud as if it were a screen. Yes, I see his small body and the soft head that fitted into my hand, his first smile, his first tooth, his sisters who held him by the hand in the living room as he took his first steps, the bruises on his legs when he came back from school, all the candles we've blown out, the summers in Brittany, his yellow slicker, the boots from André that I had gotten for him on the day he was kidnapped and that he never even tried on . . . I see his eyes full of stars when he was happy. When he was alive.

"Ilan was French," continues the ambassador, "and in his death he represents every French citizen. The French who are stunned that such a barbarous act was committed in their country."

It's true. Jean-Michel Casa is right. So many were horrified. I received hundreds of letters, from Vendée, Gironde, Lille, Marseille, Toulouse . . . I received letters that began: I'm Muslim and I'm ashamed. I'm black. I'm Catholic. I'm an atheist. I'm a mother and I'm overwhelmed. I've already said this, but I'll repeat it: I want everyone who wrote to me to know how great a comfort their words were.

"Ilan was Jewish," the ambassador finally says, "and the hatred for Jews that bred such violence forces French society to raise questions to fight the poison of anti-Semitism."

At the gathering, some are old enough to have experienced this poisonous attitude, and I can read the fear in their eyes veiled with tears. Rabbi Joseph Sitruk can't hold back his sobs either. His voice breaks when he states that this is the end of the journey. "Why Israel?" he asks, looking skywards. Why Jerusalem? Because this land is also known as *Eretz Chayim*, the "Land of Lives." *Life* in Hebrew doesn't exist in the singular. "There have always been at least two," he tells us, "this life and the other. And the reason we're here is because we believe in the other life that is beginning for Ilan.

"This, Madam, is the great lesson your son has for us. The fact that we are gathered here for him is proof of our continuing faith, proof that we remain Jews despite the trials visited upon us." I wasn't sure of that. No, I didn't know if we would still have the strength to believe . . .

We do have this strength—it's true. But maybe, it's like the man in the book *Night*, by Elie Wiesel, who looks at a child who's just been hanged and asks, "For God's sake, where is God?"

✦

We walk behind Ilan's corpse, carried by his friends. Someone holds my arms, they support me, but no one can carry my head for me; it flops to one side then the other like a dislocated puppet's. It's the end of the journey—isn't that what the great rabbi said? So I'd like to die now, immediately. I want it to be over. I advance, despite myself. I walk this last walk, spurred on by the contained anger of the vast crowd surrounding me. And, right at the end of the path, I see my son rise up into the sky, as if those who were carrying him wanted to show him to the face of the earth one last time. It looks as if he's floating like an angel, horizontally, above all these heads . . .

Yes, that's what Ilan was, a twenty-three-year-old angel whom the barbarians sacrificed for no reason. He glides from hand to hand: He's become the son and brother of all these people who press forward. The Kaddish, recited in rage, ascends, filling the air. Like so many punches, each phrase of this prayer for the dead hits the ground, the sky, everything around us. Tell us why Ilan was kidnapped, imprisoned, tied up, and gagged? Why was he beaten? Why was he starved? Why was he burned? My God, tell us why there is so much suffering . . . The pain of seeing him descend into the belly of the earth a second time makes me scream his name again.

In Hebrew, Ilan means "tree." So in his memory we decided to plant several in a forest close to Jerusalem.

Kneeling on the ground, I dig a small hole to contain the young sapling. The earth is cool, fluid, it runs through my fingers and settles under my nails. It's a fertile earth in which this "Ilan" can take root, grow, and flourish. One day its crown will touch the sky and it will bear fruit. But my son didn't have the time to bear any himself.

A Mother's Timeline

- Ilan was kidnapped on January 20, 2006, in Sceaux, and he was found close to death beside a train track in Sainte-Geneviève-des-Bois on the morning of February 13, 2006.

- He was imprisoned and tortured for twenty-four days. For the first nine days, he was kept in a vacant apartment at 1, rue Serge Prokofiev, in Bagneux, then in the boiler room of a neighboring building.

- While he was imprisoned we received about seven hundred phone calls, three photographs, and two audio recordings.

- Initially, the kidnappers asked us to pay a ransom of 450,000 euros for his release, but the amount changed all the time. In the end, they asked only for 5,000 euros.

✦ During this period the police had several opportunities to arrest Youssouf Fofana, the ringleader of the "Gang of Barbarians."

✦ The autopsy shows burn marks covering 80 percent of Ilan's body, numerous bruises and contusions, a nearly three-inch-long incision made with a blade along his left cheek, as well as two stab wounds below his throat. The medical examiner concluded that none of the stab wounds was fatal. His death was the result of the overall effect of the torture, exhaustion, and cold to which he was subjected.

✦ Before Ilan, five other Jews—Orville Aubert, Jaimie Garnier, Martin Durand, Jacques Durand, and Maurice Keller—escaped the "Gang of Barbarians" by the skin of their teeth. This criminal gang also targeted doctors and lawyers of the Jewish faith: In 2005 doctors and lawyers had been the victims of a blackmailing racket.

✦ In all, twenty-nine suspects were taken into custody for "associating with criminals, kidnapping, sequestration as an organized gang, acts of torture and barbarism and assassination." Of the twenty-nine people arrested, several are still in prison today.

✦ Fofana was sentenced to life in prison with no possibility of parole for twenty-two years. His two most active accomplices received sentences of up to eighteen years in prison. Others involved in the crime were sentenced to between six months and nine years in prison. Two defendants were acquitted.

A Note from the Coauthor

I LEARNED ABOUT Ilan Halimi's assassination like everyone else, from a snippet in the press. It described a young, twenty-three-year-old man who had been found dying beside a railroad track. And then, a few days later, I saw a photo of him. I discovered that he had been kidnapped, held hostage for three weeks, tortured, and then dumped in the woods. A sordid tale, I thought, just a terrible anecdote. But you tend to forget anecdotes, and I was about to forget this one when I heard Ilan's mother on RTL radio: "My son was sacrificed in the name of all young Jews. If he hadn't been Jewish, he wouldn't have been murdered."

I will never forget these two sentences. I was alone in my car, and it was as if time had stopped.

I switched off the radio and went home. I shut myself up in my apartment. I avidly read the press, devouring everything I could find about Ilan, his ordeal, his torturers. I wanted to understand, just understand, what could have been going on in the minds of these kids, how something like this could have happened . . . And I wrote *La Mort d'un Pote* (the English translation would be *A Pal's Death* [Panama, 2006]). At the time, this book wasn't about what had happened to Ilan—I knew little about that, just what I had learned from the media—but it described the background against which this horrific kidnapping took place, France of the early 2000s. When it was released, I sent Ilan's parents a copy. I just had to send it to them, but I also feared their reaction. I would have found it unbearable if it had hurt them, with all they'd already endured . . .

Ruth called me. She had read *La Mort d'un Pote*, and she wanted us to have lunch. I met her, a small woman full of life, just outside her office. She smiled at me as if we'd known each other for years. I was on the verge of tears. I couldn't speak or hold back the tears that were already blurring my vision. She thanked me. I had done nothing more than write what I thought, but she shared my viewpoint. It was what she would have wanted to say; my words had helped a bit . . . We spent a short hour together, and she was the one who comforted me, who told me I had to be strong, I should never break down, never give up. Never give up, she repeated, borrowing the words from a foreign journalist who was stunned that anti-Semitism could be rearing its head again in France.

This woman's courage was a great lesson to me. And more than her courage, I was overwhelmed by her unwavering faith in the goodness of humankind. To continue to believe in humanity after all she had been through was an act of heroism. So when she asked me to write a book with her, to record the facts, to describe what Ilan had suffered so that he would never be forgotten, and so that nothing as barbaric as this could ever happen again, I only did what I had to. Never give up.

Émilie Frèche

A Note from the Translator

The day I was to meet Mrs. Halimi I was apprehensive. What do you say to someone who has lost her son under such terrible circumstances? What words are there that could possibly mean anything?

We met in the street and walked to a crowded restaurant. Within minutes I realized that Mrs. Halimi does not carry her story with her like a stigma. She is a joyful, warm, generous lady, who lives in the present. Her eyes twinkle when she talks about her grandchildren. She is attentive to the world around her. Over the meal, we talked about the possibilities of finding a publisher for the translated book. She spoke of the many conferences she had attended all over the world to speak against hatred and prejudice.

As we left each other on the sidewalk, she hugged me and said, "I don't want this book to be a 'Jewish' book. I don't hate anyone; that would be futile. It's not only Ilan's story. I want it to be published to remind people of what hatred and intolerance can do, hatred for the Other, intolerance of what we see as different. Given the world we live in today, we have to remember that we are all people, and we are the same, regardless of our beliefs. Otherwise, there will be very dark times ahead."

In this spirit, I believe this book has its place in the world. It recounts Ilan's ordeal and how his family suffered for weeks, hoping their son would return. It describes how dozens of people were involved at different levels, but none of them spoke out. No one tried to put a stop to this violence. Ilan could have been anyone's son; his kidnapping was a mercenary act of hatred against a community perceived as wealthy. But as intolerance grows, acts of hatred and violence could target anyone, any community in our increasingly globalized world.

Renuka George

Library of Congress Cataloging-in-Publication Data

Names: Halimi, Ruth, author. | Frèche, Émilie, author. | George, Renuka, translator.

Title: 24 days : the kidnapping and murder of Ilan Halimi / Ruth Halimi, Émilie Frèche ; translated by Renuka George ; foreword by Jonathan Greenblatt, Anti-Defamation League.

Other titles: 24 jours. English | Twenty-four days

Description: Millburn, New Jersey : Behrman House, 2020. | Summary: "On January 20, 2006, Ilan Halimi, chosen because he was Jewish, was kidnapped and taken to an apartment in Bagneux. He was held and tortured there for three weeks before being thrown into the woods by his executioners. Found naked along the Sainte-Geneviève-des-Bois rail, he did not survive his ordeal. In this poignant memoir, Ruth Halimi, Ilan's mother, recalls the twenty-four days of this nightmare. Twenty-four days during which she received over 600 phone calls, ransom demands that constantly changed, insults, threats, and pictures of her tortured son. Police procedures repeatedly failed. The case was eventually solved and a gang of suburban hoodlums (who later earned the name of "le Gang des Barbares"), led by an Ivorian immigrant, Youssouf Fofana, were arrested by police. What shocked the public at the time was that Fofana and his gang members claimed openly that they thought Jews were usually wealthy and united, and for these reasons they imagined the Jewish community would pull together to pay a large ransom for Halimi's release. The US edition-a joint publication of Behrman House Inc and the Anti-Defamation League (ADL)-includes a new foreword and modern-day anti-Semitic news vignettes to show the universal problem of anti-Semitism"-- Provided by publisher.

Identifiers: LCCN 2019028418 | ISBN 9781681150086 (hardcover) | ISBN 9781681150505 (kindle edition)

Subjects: LCSH: Halimi, Ilan, -2006. | Victims of hate crimes--France. | Hate crimes--France. | Antisemitism--France.

Classification: LCC HV6773.55.F8 H3513 2020 | DDC 364.152/3092--dc23

LC record available at https://lccn.loc.gov/2019028418